From Falling Behind to Catching Up

DIRECTIONS IN DEVELOPMENT
Public Sector Governance

From Falling Behind to Catching Up

A Country Economic Memorandum for Malawi

Richard Record, Praveen Kumar, and Priscilla Kandoole

Contents

Boxes

Figures

Tables

About the Authors

Richard Record is a Senior Economist in the World Bank Group Macroeconomics and Fiscal Management Global Practice. Based in Lilongwe, Malawi, he manages the World Bank's engagement on economic policy issues, including publication of the flagship *Malawi Economic Monitor*. Before moving to the Africa region, Richard worked in the Southeast Asia Unit, based in Vientiane, Lao People's Democratic Republic, managing programs on macroeconomics, trade, and private sector development. He has a BSc in economics from the London School of Economics, an MSc in economics from the School of Oriental and Africa Studies, and a PhD in development economics from the University of Manchester.

Praveen Kumar is an Economic Adviser in the World Bank, mapped to the Macroeconomics and Fiscal Management Global Practice. He has extensive experience in preparing economic reports for the governments in Eastern Africa, South Asia, and Middle East and Northern Africa. His areas of expertise are macroeconomic policy, economic growth, fiscal management, public sector, and labor markets. He has a B. Tech in mechanical engineering from the Indian Institute of Technology, New Delhi, an M. Tech in Systems and Management from the Indian Institute of Technology, New Delhi, and a PhD in economics from the University of Maryland, College Park.

Priscilla Kandoole is an economist in the World Bank Group's Macroeconomics and Fiscal Management Global Practice. She manages and contributes to analytical tasks, reform support operations, and economic monitoring as part of the economic work program in Malawi. This includes biannual publication of the flagship *Malawi Economic Monitor*, as well as economic modeling and forecasting. Previously, Priscilla worked as a Principal Economist in the Ministry of Finance, Economic Planning and Development in Malawi, focusing on macroeconomic accounting, analysis, policy, and research. She has a BSc in economics from the University of Malawi–Chancellor College and an MSc in international economics and finance from the University of Queensland.

Acknowledgments

This Country Economic Memorandum (CEM) was prepared by a World Bank team led by Richard Record and Praveen Kumar, with assistance from Priscilla Kandoole, Eleni Stylianou, and Sunganani Kalemba. The overview report was put together by Richard Record, Praveen Kumar, and Minna Hahn Tong, based on background papers prepared as part of the CEM process, with contributions by Bill Battaile, Todd Benson, Kate Bridges, Tillmann von Carnap, Efrem Chilima, George Clarke, Brent Edelman, Leonardo Garrido, Ejaz Ghani, Carter Hemphill, Priscilla Kandoole, Katie Kibuuka, Christian Ksoll, Charles Kunaka, Winford Masanjala, Tuan Minh Le, Brian Pinto, Eleni Stylianou, Carlos Vicente, and Shahid Yusuf. The team wishes to thank Bob Baulch, Kevin Carey, Åsa Giertz, Lucy Hayes, Deborah Isser, Thomas Munthali, Ben Musuku, Roisin Parish, and Yutaka Yoshino as well as peer reviewers Luc Christiaensen, Nick Lea, Khwima Nthara, and Shomikho Raha for their constructive input. Administrative and report production assistance from Lydie Ahodehou, Zeria Banda, and Deliwe Ziyandammanja is gratefully acknowledged. Overall guidance was provided by Abebe Adugna, Laura Kullenberg, and Bella Bird.

The report greatly benefited from many interactions with stakeholders in Malawi, including principally management and staff of the Department of Economic Planning and Development as well as several other departments in the Ministry of Finance, Economic Planning, and Development; the Reserve Bank of Malawi; the National Statistical Office; the Ministry of Agriculture, Irrigation, and Water Development; the Ministry of Industry, Trade, and Tourism; the Malawi Revenue Authority; and other government ministries, departments, and agencies. The team would also like to thank representatives of the private sector in Blantyre and Lilongwe for their helpful feedback and contributions, as well as Malawi's community of development partners.

The CEM was prepared in close partnership with the United States Agency for International Development and the United Kingdom Department for International Development.

The findings and interpretations expressed here are those of the authors and do not necessarily reflect the views of the World Bank Group, its executive directors, or the countries they represent.

Abbreviations

ADMARC	Agricultural Development and Marketing Corporation
CEM	Country Economic Memorandum
FISP	Farm Input Subsidy Program
GDP	gross domestic product
HIPC	Highly Indebted Poor Countries
MDRI	Multilateral Debt Relief Initiative
NFRA	National Food Reserve Agency
ODA	official development assistance
PPP	purchasing power parity
SAFEX	South African Futures Exchange
TFP	total factor productivity

CHAPTER 1

The Puzzle of Malawi's Lack of Development

Despite decades of development efforts supported by significant amounts of foreign aid, Malawi has experienced weak and volatile economic growth over a sustained period of time and has fallen behind its peers. Malawi's real per capita gross domestic product (GDP) grew at an average of around 1.5 percent between 1995 and 2015, falling below the average of 2.67 percent in non-resource-rich Sub-Saharan African economies over the last 20 years. Malawi's growth remains an outlier even compared with that of its geographically and demographically similar peers that were at a similar stage of development in 1990 (figure 1.1). Malawi's growth has also been relatively volatile, with the size of fluctuations in growth per capita remaining persistently higher than the regional average since the country's independence.

Moreover, growth has been distributed unequally, with little impact on poverty. Per capita income has improved only minimally in the 50 years since Malawi's independence, and Malawi now has one of the lowest per capita incomes in the world. It is therefore not surprising that recent poverty headcounts, based on Integrated Household Survey data, show that poverty in Malawi remained stagnant at more than 50 percent and actually increased in rural areas between 2004 and 2011. Based on a cross-country comparison for 2010, Malawi was one of the poorest countries in the world, with 77.3 percent of its population living below US$1.90 per day. Moreover, it appears that whatever growth occurred was not distributed evenly across rural and urban areas and across wealth levels: between 2004 and 2011, per capita consumption declined for more than 60 percent of the rural population while increasing for almost the entire urban population (especially for those at the higher end).

Given that several important factors have been working in Malawi's favor, the lack of progress in growth and poverty reduction is puzzling. Malawi's low and volatile growth performance relative to that of its peers is particularly striking given that Malawi has stayed politically stable and free of conflicts and has suffered no more weather-related or other external shocks than other countries

Figure 1.1 Growth of Real per Capita GDP in Malawi and Selected Benchmark Countries in Sub-Saharan Africa, 1990–2015

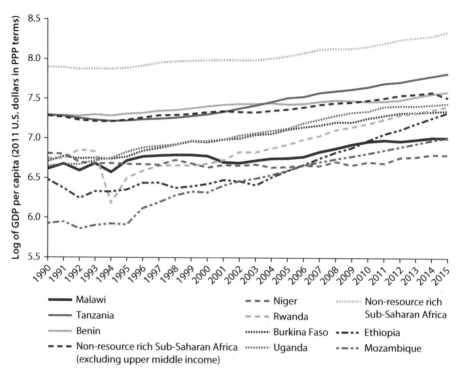

Source: Kandoole, Stylianou, and von Carnap 2016.
Note: GDP = gross domestic product; PPP = purchasing power parity.

in the region. Some countries such as Mozambique and Rwanda have faced even more difficult conditions, needing to rebuild their nations after violent conflict, yet still have managed to achieve higher and more sustained growth than Malawi (Kandoole, Stylianou, and von Carnap 2016). Moreover, contrary to empirical research showing that democracy leads to greater stability in economic performance in most countries (Rodrik 2000), the volatility of Malawi's growth did not decline much after the introduction of multiparty democracy in 1994.

This new Country Economic Memorandum (CEM), prepared at the request of the government of Malawi, aims to improve understanding of the puzzle of Malawi's weak performance and to identify ways for Malawi to achieve robust and stable growth that includes the poor. The government plans to use the CEM to inform the preparation of a new Growth and Development Strategy document that will succeed the Malawi Growth and Development Strategy II. As in the past, the CEM is also expected to influence the national debate on policy matters and the aid programs of international development partners. Within the World Bank, the work carried out for the CEM will be used to support preparation of the Systematic Country Diagnostic, in conjunction with a new Poverty Assessment for Malawi.

Notably, this CEM differs from previous CEMs in several ways. First, it assesses Malawi's growth experience since independence from a comparative international perspective,[1] benchmarks Malawian outcomes on growth, structural change, and transformation against those of its peers and other Sub-Saharan African countries, and explores possible reasons for divergence from international trends. Second, it puts deeper drivers of economic growth at the center of the discussion, looking in particular at the institutions and policies that may have affected Malawi's growth outcomes and the ones that could help Malawi to avoid macroeconomic instability in the future (box 1.1).

The CEM also uses new data to analyze policies to support growth in agricultural productivity and in private enterprises (especially in urban areas). The analysis of agricultural productivity draws on the considerable volume of new analysis and information available on the impact of recent economic and sectoral policies,

---

Box 1.1 Understanding the Deeper Determinants of Growth in Malawi

The empirical literature on long-run economic growth has come to differentiate between proximate determinants of growth, such as accumulation of physical and human capital, and deeper determinants, such as geography and institutions (Rodrik 2003). Over very long periods of time, deeper determinants empirically explain growth outcomes better. Hsieh and Klenow (2010) summarize the research on international differences in income across countries with reference to the following chain of causality:

Geography, climate, luck $\rightarrow$ human capital, physical capital, TFP $\rightarrow$ income
$\downarrow$
Institutions, culture $\rightarrow$ human capital, physical capital, TFP $\rightarrow$ income
$\downarrow$
Policies, rule of law, corruption $\rightarrow$ human capital, physical capital, TFP $\rightarrow$ income.

As this chain of causality depicts, besides geography and other factors, institutions and policies (including rule of law) can constitute deeper forces affecting the accumulation of human and physical capital and TFP growth (all of which are proximate determinants of income) across countries.

This Country Economic Memorandum (CEM) probes into the factors that may be deeper determinants of growth for Malawi, particularly in the area of institutions and policies. The CEM establishes that the main proximate reason for low growth rates in Malawi has been low physical capital accumulation. The main factor behind low investment has been considerable macroeconomic instability due to the inability of the government to manage shocks as well as several policy-induced shocks. The analysis then delves deeper into political economy and institutional issues behind the lapses in macroeconomic management. Two questions related to institutions are examined: first, what kind of fiscal institutions will enable Malawi to avoid the fiscal slippages that have been behind the bouts of macroeconomic instability, and second, why have institutional reforms often failed to deliver the intended outcomes?

Note: TFP = total factor productivity.

---

particularly those surrounding initiatives such as the Farm Input Subsidy Program. Similarly, the analysis of enterprise productivity draws on recent Enterprise Survey data that have not been analyzed previously.

The CEM has been prepared by a joint team of government and development partners employing a strong collaborative and "learning by doing" approach. The joint task team included staff from the International Food Policy Research Institute, United Kingdom Department for International Development, United States Agency for International Development, and World Bank, working alongside a small counterpart team from Malawi's Ministry of Finance, Economic Planning, and Development. This inclusive and open approach was adopted with the aim of engaging with counterparts and policy makers on difficult development issues in a pragmatic way. It included a series of "knowledge and learning events" undertaken during the course of CEM preparation, in which team members shared key research questions and early findings for feedback, guidance, and validation.

This book summarizes and consolidates the extensive background technical work conducted for the CEM. It is structured as follows. First, it discusses Malawi's macroeconomic situation and challenges in fiscal management, reviewing and drawing lessons from the instability, slippages, and shocks that Malawi has experienced since independence. Second, given how critical the agriculture sector is to poverty reduction in Malawi, it explores the current state of agricultural markets. Third, it looks at the factors that may constrain higher growth in the future and discusses challenges in private sector development and job creation. Finally, building on the analysis of challenges, the overview concludes with a summary of policy recommendations aimed at helping Malawi to achieve more robust and sustainable growth and poverty reduction in the future. The full list of background papers, each of which is available for download, is provided as appendix A to this book.

Note

1. The previous two CEMs in Malawi also focused on growth; the last one was completed in 2010 and the previous one in 2004. The 2010 CEM covered developments up until the end of 2008.

References

Hsieh, C., and P. Klenow. 2010. "Development Accounting." *American Economic Journal: Macroeconomics* 2 (1): 207–23.

Kandoole, P., E. Stylianou, and T. von Carnap. 2016. "Malawi's Growth Performance in a Historical Perspective: Implications for Future Growth Strategy." Malawi Country Economic Memorandum background paper, World Bank, Washington, DC.

Rodrik, D. 2000. "Participatory Politics, Social Cooperation, and Economic Stability." *American Economic Review* 90 (2): 140–44.

———. 2003. "Institutions, Integration, and Geography: In Search of the Deep Determinants of Economic Growth." In *Search of Prosperity: Analytic Country Studies on Growth*, edited by D. Rodrik. Princeton, NJ: Princeton University Press.

CHAPTER 2

The Importance of Macroeconomic Stability and Fiscal Management

At the time of the country's independence in 1964, it was hoped that Malawi would make rapid progress from its low level of economic development. At that time, with a per capita gross domestic product (GDP) of US$242 (in constant 2010 terms), Malawi was the poorest of the three territories in the Central African Federation.[1] It had almost no mineral resources, limited infrastructure, and a largely subsistence agrarian economy that was frequently hit by weather shocks. Moreover, the country depended heavily on external skills and capital. Domestic savings were virtually nonexistent, and government recurrent budget deficits were met by grants-in-aid from the United Kingdom. Malawi also faced major human development challenges, with low school enrollment rates and poor quality of education. Nonetheless, there was hope that the country's development would accelerate after independence since it could make choices about development for the common good of Malawians rather than following the choices of the colonial powers.

Yet more than 50 years later, Malawi has barely progressed. The country's GDP per capita in 2015 was US$494 (in constant 2010 terms), only slightly higher than double what it was at independence. Around 56.6 percent of the rural population and 17.3 percent of the urban population lived in poverty in fiscal year 2010/11, and the economy remains predominantly dependent on agriculture. As discussed in greater detail in this chapter, Malawi's performance has diverged even from the generally mediocre performance of Sub-Saharan African economies over this long period, despite the fact that Malawi has remained politically stable and free of conflicts, while many African economies have experienced instability and conflict. This divergence has become particularly pronounced in the past two decades.

Malawi's relative lack of progress over more than half a century calls for a closer examination of its economic history and an analysis of the factors affecting its growth and development performance. This chapter begins with an overview of growth trends since independence, describing Malawi's performance in the area of GDP growth, poverty reduction and human development, and structural change and putting it into a comparative perspective. Malawi's growth experience is also broken down into different periods to identify changes over time and examine sources of growth. The chapter then discusses macroeconomic volatility and the reasons behind it, looking at external shocks and the policy responses that accompanied them as well as policy-induced shocks. Finally, recognizing the central importance of fiscal management in driving macroeconomic stability in Malawi, it concludes with an assessment of fiscal management over time.

Growth and Poverty Trends since Independence

Economic growth is the most appropriate measure of economic performance for low- and middle-income economies like Malawi. Expressed in GDP per capita terms, economic growth measures the pace of improvement in living standards of residents. Growth is also an indicator of how rapidly poverty might be falling—empirical evidence shows that poverty reduction across countries is correlated with GDP growth (Dollar and Kraay 2002). Finally, growth can capture the structural change taking place in the economy. All three of these measures are discussed in this section.

GDP Growth

Like the rest of Africa, Malawi has experienced periods of growth acceleration and collapse. Table 2.1 breaks Malawi's economic growth since independence into five periods[2]: (a) rapid growth from 1964 until 1979; (b) economic decline from 1980 to 1994; (c) periodic episodes of growth from 1995 until 2002, generally characterized by high levels of volatility; (d) strong growth from 2003 to 2010; and (e) collapse of growth and stagnation from 2011 to 2015. This breakdown by period shows relatively sharp differences across period averages, with average growth of GDP per capita ranging from 3.65 percent during 1964–79 to −1.76 percent during 1980–94.

Table 2.1 Economic Growth in Malawi since Independence, 1964–2015

Indicator	1964–79	1980–94	1995–2002	2003–10	2011–15
GDP per capita: start of period	241.55	407.16	367.81	369.75	479.25
GDP per capita: end of period	417.47	318.25	358.74	471.21	494.41
GDP per capita growth (%)	3.65	−1.76	−0.36	3.46	0.78
GDP growth (%)	6.40	1.50	2.25	6.32	3.85
Standard deviation of GDP per capita growth	4.75	5.45	6.64	1.89	1.57

Source: Estimates based on World Development Indicators data.
Note: GDP = gross domestic product. GDP per capita is real GDP per capita in constant 2010 U.S. dollars.

Although Malawi's periods of growth acceleration and collapse broadly mimic those at the overall level in Sub-Saharan Africa, the pace of growth has diverged noticeably since 1980. Overall consistencies between Malawi's performance and that of the Sub-Saharan region more broadly suggest the existence of regional drivers of these movements over long periods (Go and Page 2008). However, the juxtaposition of Malawi's performance vis-à-vis the rest of Sub-Saharan Africa across three periods since independence also shows divergence in their growth trends (figure 2.1). Malawi's per capita GDP grew relatively rapidly—at 3.65 percent a year on average—during the first 15 years after independence, allowing it to move closer to average GDP for the rest of Sub-Saharan Africa. However, it shrunk much faster than in the rest of Sub-Saharan Africa during 1980–94, when the rest of Africa also suffered a decline in living standards. Furthermore, while GDP per capita for the rest of Sub-Saharan Africa grew at a decent average of 2.9 percent per year after 1995, Malawi's growth was much lower at 1.48 percent. Out of 45 Sub-Saharan African economies, Malawi ranked 15 in average growth between 1964 and 1994 and ranked 23 between 1995 and 2015.

Moreover, Malawi's real per capita growth has fallen behind that of most of its peers.[3] In 1990, Malawi's level of development was similar to that of Burkina Faso, Ethiopia, Rwanda, and Uganda. By 2015, all peer countries (with the exception of Niger) had experienced economic growth, reaching higher levels of real GDP per capita than in 1990, with signs of convergence among these countries. In contrast, Malawi experienced much lower economic development. Even Mozambique, which had less than half the level of GDP per capita in purchasing power parity (PPP) terms as Malawi in 1990, managed to reach a similar level as Malawi by 2015.

Figure 2.1 Growth of Real GDP per Capita in Malawi and Sub-Saharan Africa, 1964–2015

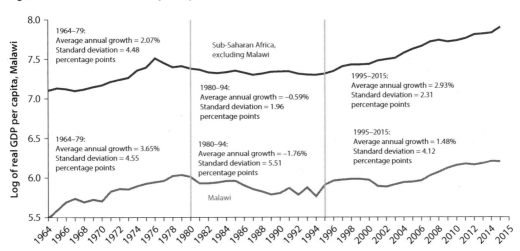

Source: Kandoole, Stylianou, and von Carnap 2016.
Note: GDP = gross domestic product. Real GDP per capita is GDP per capita in constant 2010 U.S. dollars.

Poverty Reduction and Human Development

Associated with slow growth, Malawi has had mixed success in poverty reduction. Somewhat encouragingly, noticeable gains have been made in nonmonetary measures of poverty. For example, the rate of enrollment in primary education has risen steadily, with the proportion of school-age children attending primary school increasing from 53 percent in 2004 to 61 percent in 2013. Similarly, the rate of under-five infant mortality has also declined from 133 deaths per 1,000 live births in 2004 to 64 deaths in 2015. With these gains as well as others, Malawi has attained four of eight Millennium Development Goals. However, improvements on such measures of human development have been uneven and skewed toward the high-income percentiles, with little or marginal gains for the bottom 40 percent. Moreover, progress on monetary poverty has remained elusive (Dabalen and others 2017) and even increased over the period for which comparable data are available (1997–2011).

Poverty has remained stubbornly high, particularly in rural Malawi, where 85 percent of the population resides. Data from household Living Standards Measurement Surveys show that urban poverty fell from 25.4 percent of the urban population in 2004 to 17.3 percent in 2010, while rural poverty increased slightly from 55.9 to 56.6 percent (figure 2.2). During the same period, poverty became more entrenched, as both the depth (how far the poor are from the poverty line) and severity (share of households that are below the poverty line) of poverty increased by 1.1 percentage points at the national level (figure 2.3). This increase was driven by rural areas. The number of people living in poverty also increased in absolute terms from 11.2 million in 2004 to 12.9 million in 2010, partly due to high population growth as well as the uneven distribution of

Figure 2.2 Household Poverty Rates in Malawi, by Rural–Urban Location, 2004 and 2010

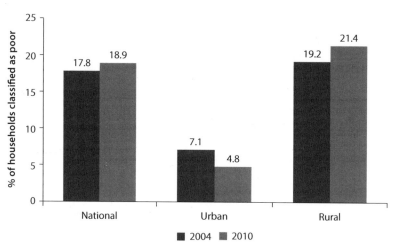

Source: Calculations based on data from the second and third Integrated Household Surveys.

Figure 2.3 Depth of Poverty in Malawi, by Rural–Urban Location, 2004 and 2010

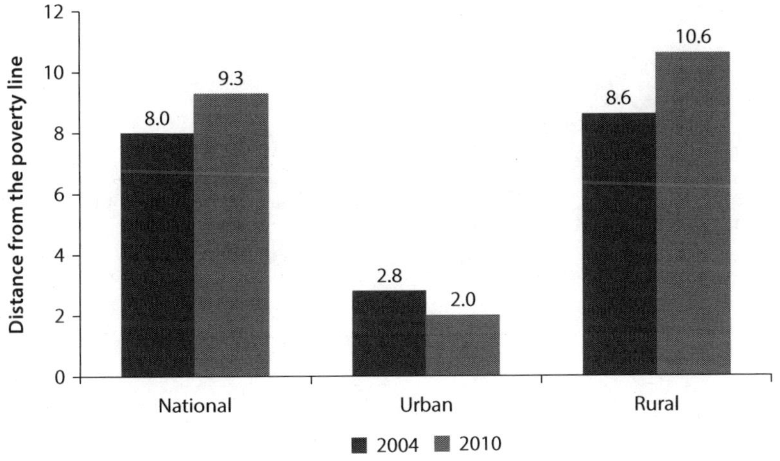

Source: Calculations based on data from the second and third Integrated Household Surveys.

economic growth. During this period, the Gini coefficient (a measure of income inequality) increased from 39.87 to 46.12. At the same time, the share of consumption claimed by the bottom 40 percent fell from 18 percent in 2004 to 15 percent in 2010.

Currently, poverty incidence in Malawi is one of the highest among low-income Sub-Saharan African countries (figure 2.4). Using an internationally comparative measure—the US$1.90 a day poverty line at 2011 PPP—approximately 71 percent of Malawians were living below the poverty line in 2010, a meager 2.7 percent decline from 73.6 percent in 2004. Using Malawi's own poverty line, the poverty headcount declined marginally from 52.7 percent in 2004 to 50.7 percent in 2010.

Moreover, despite the gains that have been achieved, Malawi's basic level of human development remains extremely low, undermining future prospects for growth. Persistently high rates of malnutrition, with around half (46 percent) of children in the poorest quintile suffering from chronic malnutrition, have long-term effects on learning and the building of human capital. Added to a weak base of human capital is the heavy burden of disease, particularly human immunodeficiency virus/acquired immunodeficiency syndrome and malaria.

The accumulated evidence suggests three proximate causes for the stagnant poverty levels in Malawi (Dabalen and others 2017). First, the level of productivity in agriculture—which is the main economic activity for the bulk of the poor—has remained low. Second, opportunities for nonfarm self-employment in rural areas are limited, and the returns on such activities are relatively low, especially for the poor. Third, the government's major safety net programs have had only a limited impact on poverty, mainly due to limited coverage rates and poor targeting (World Bank 2016).

Figure 2.4 Poverty Rates in Malawi and Other Sub-Saharan African Countries, Various Years

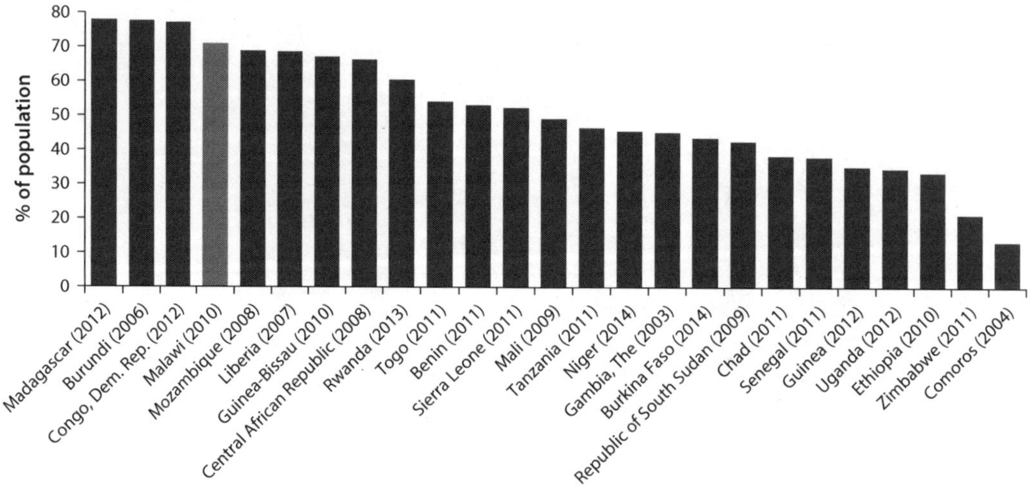

Source: Calculations based on World Development Indicators data.
Note: International poverty line at US$1.90 a day (in 2011 PPP terms); PPP = purchasing power parity.

Structural Change

Throughout much of Malawi's postindependence history, the structure of the economy changed very little. Malawi developed a highly dualistic agriculture sector, with tight controls and a wide gap between the capital-intensive estate sector and the subsistence smallholder sector. A highly interventionist state attempted to guide the allocation of capital and large swathes of economic activity. While structural adjustment reforms in the 1980s and 1990s, accompanied by Malawi's transition to democracy, brought progressive liberalization and a rollback of the formal state, many of Malawi's statist institutions, such as the Agricultural Development and Marketing Corporation (ADMARC), have persisted.

Since 2000, positive yet limited structural transformation appears to have been taking place. In the context of development, the move from agriculture to more productive sectors is usually seen as a precondition for attaining higher incomes and higher overall productivity. Over the past two decades, labor in Malawi has shifted gradually, with the share of agriculture decreasing to around 30 percent of GDP and that of services growing to contribute more than half of economic output (Enache, Ghani, and O'Connell 2016). The speed of transformation has been relatively slow, especially in the context of Malawi's rapidly growing population.

Notably, labor has been shifting toward sectors in which productivity is declining over time. Wholesale and retail trade has had the highest increase in employment share, followed by government services and construction. These sectors have also been among the least productive, with negative growth of sectoral value added per worker, although with higher productivity than agriculture.

Figure 2.5 Changes in Sectoral Productivity and Employment Shares in Malawi, 1970–90 and 1990–2010

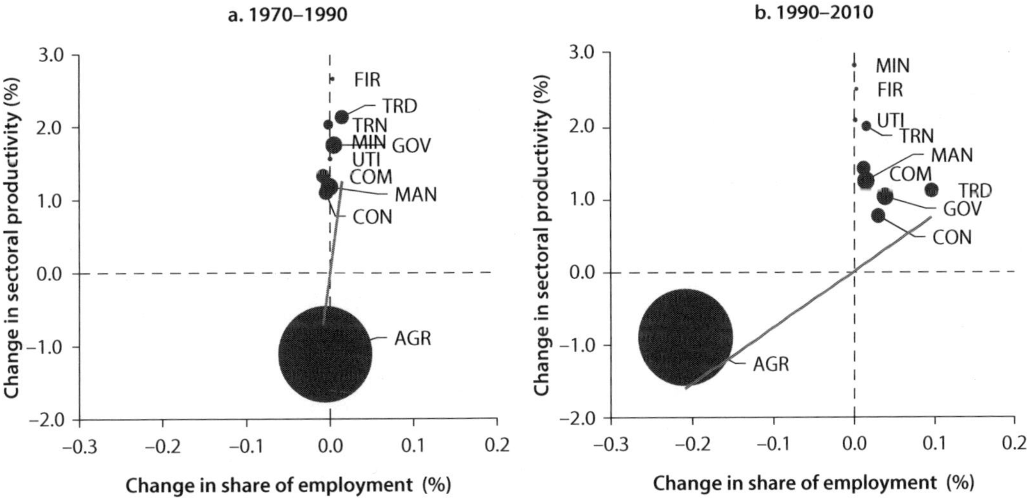

a. 1970–1990

b. 1990–2010

Source: Enache, Ghani, and O'Connell 2016.
Note: AGR = agriculture; COM = communications; CON = construction; FIR = financial and business services; GOV = government; MAN = manufacturing; MIN = mining; TRD = trade services; TRN = transport and communications; UTL = utilities. The size of the bubble indicates the share of employment in the sector at the beginning of the period.

The movement of workers to sectors with declining productivity suggests that employment growth has been the result of "push" factors out of agriculture (for example, population pressures, degradation of soils) rather than "pull" factors into services. Relatively productive sectors such as mining, business services, transport, and public utilities have thus far failed to provide a significant number of jobs and only marginally increased their share of employment (figure 2.5).

Notably, Malawi has not experienced any major expansion in the industrial sector, which has been a key driver of transformation in other (particularly Asian) low- and middle-income economies. Moreover, the evidence suggests that capital-intensive enterprises have developed in the "wrong" sectors, resulting in minimal improvement in competitiveness and creating very little employment.

Despite these shifts, agriculture continues to be the dominant sector with regard to both its share of GDP and the number of people employed. Agriculture remains the main source of Malawi's economic growth, contributing around three-quarters of total export earnings and employing around 64 percent of the labor force (NSO 2014).

Sources of Growth

With respect to the factors that have been driving Malawi's development, labor has generally become a more significant source of growth over time. This section uses a standard growth accounting approach to decompose historical growth of income into growth of factors of production—namely, physical and human capital.[4] As shown in table 2.2, the contribution of labor has remained positive and relatively significant over time.

A large share of GDP growth can also be ascribed to total factor productivity (TFP) growth. As shown in table 2.2, during the period of strong GDP growth from 2003 to 2010, TFP was the most significant contributor to GDP growth, followed closely by labor. Even after taking into account the growth in human capital (thanks to increased schooling and educational attainment among Malawi's labor force, particularly since the 1990s), periods of high economic growth have also been periods of high TFP growth.[5] In fact, TFP growth closely tracks GDP per capita growth (figure 2.6).

In contrast, the contribution of physical capital to economic growth has been quite small since 1980, with the rate of capital accumulation falling far behind labor growth. While the contribution of physical capital to economic growth was

Table 2.2 Contribution of Labor and TFP Growth to Real GDP Growth in Malawi, 1964–2015
Percent

Component	1964–79	1980–94	1995–2002	2003–10	2011–15
GDP growth	8.79	0.90	2.85	6.25	3.82
Total factor productivity	2.68	−1.46	2.14	2.59	1.55
Physical capital	4.62	0.69	0.07	1.09	0.24
Labor	1.49	1.68	0.63	2.57	2.03

Sources: Estimates based on Penn World Tables 9.0 data for 1964–2014; for 2015, real GDP growth based on World Development Indicators data and employment growth based on International Labour Organization data.
Note: GDP = gross domestic product; TFP = total factor productivity.

Figure 2.6 TFP Growth and Real per Capita GDP in Malawi, 1965–2015

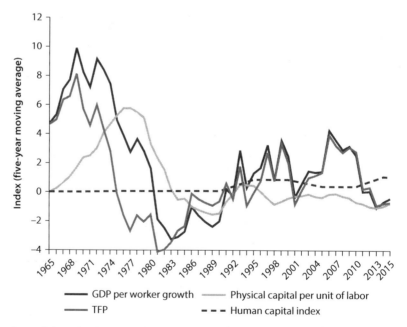

Sources: Estimates based on Penn World Tables 9.0 data for 1964–2014; for 2015, real GDP growth based on World Development Indicators data and employment growth based on International Labour Organization data.
Note: GDP = gross domestic product; TFP = total factor productivity.

significant during the high-growth period of 1964–79, its contribution has fallen dramatically since then (table 2.2). In fact, when taking into account population growth by looking at the contribution of physical capital per worker, it appears that physical capital per worker has contributed negatively to economic growth in Malawi since 1980 (table 2.3). This shows that the rate of capital accumulation has lagged far behind labor growth, resulting in thinning of the capital base of the economy.

These findings suggest that the failure to deepen its physical capital stock has been the proximate reason behind Malawi's inability to grow faster. Capital stock per worker has been declining since around 1980 and remained almost stagnant since 1990. The inability to grow the capital stock has been somewhat specific to Malawi compared with its Sub-Saharan African peers (figure 2.7), so the reasons behind it are also likely to be specific to Malawi.

Table 2.3 Contribution of Physical Capital per Worker to Economic Growth in Malawi, 1964–2015

Percent

Component	1964–79	1980–94	1995–2002	2003–10	2011–15
GDP per worker growth	6.29	−1.92	1.78	1.92	0.40
Total factor productivity	2.68	−1.46	2.14	2.59	1.55
Physical capital per unit of labor	3.60	−0.46	−0.36	−0.67	−1.15

Sources: Estimates based on Penn World Tables 9.0 data for 1964–2014; for 2015, real GDP growth based on World Development Indicators data and employment growth based on International Labour Organization data.
Note: GDP = gross domestic product.

Figure 2.7 Capital Stock in Malawi and Select Sub-Saharan African Countries, 1964–2015

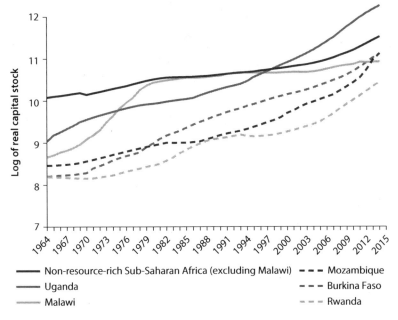

Source: Estimates based on Penn World Tables 9.0 data.

The stagnation in capital accumulation over such a long period of time is mostly attributed to macroeconomic volatility. In recent years, economists have used a methodology called growth diagnostics, developed by Hausmann, Rodrik, and Velasco (2005), to identify constraints to private investment in a country. This approach systematically looks at evidence on constraints to the demand for investment and the supply of investment finance to identify reasons behind low investment rates. Drawing on that approach, there is a compelling argument that private investment has been low in Malawi due to low expected returns to economic activity, which in turn have been low due to macroeconomic instability. The frequent bouts of macroeconomic instability in Malawi are discussed in greater detail next.

Macroeconomic Instability and Its Causes

Malawi's history since independence is characterized by repeated episodes of macroeconomic instability. These episodes have involved a combination of macroeconomic policy variables and outcomes traditionally associated with instability: growth collapses, high inflation, low international reserves, currency depreciation, and large fiscal deficits (figures 2.8–2.11). During the period 1992–2015, seven such episodes of varying duration took place (table 2.4).

Such macroeconomic instability has implications for Malawi's long-run growth and poverty reduction. Frequent bouts of macroeconomic instability have contributed to Malawi's fall in long-run growth compared with that of its peers in Sub-Saharan Africa, whose long-run growth since the mid-1990s is partly explained by their stable macroeconomic situations. Overall macroeconomic instability could also be an important factor behind the persistently high incidence of poverty in Malawi. Apart from the indirect effect through slower growth, instability directly hurts the poor. Empirical evidence suggests that lower inflation is associated with greater improvements in the welfare of the poor (Easterly and Fischer 2001). Moreover, as argued in the *World Development Report 2000/2001*, macroeconomic crises tend to be associated with increases in income poverty and inequality, and such increases in poverty may not be reversed once the crises end (World Bank 2001).

A common assumption is that the recurring and drawn-out episodes of macroeconomic instability are due to Malawi's relatively frequent external shocks. Indeed, as a small, open economy with an undiversified base of production and exports and a heavy dependence on aid, Malawi is vulnerable to weather shocks such as droughts and floods, terms-of-trade shocks such as oil and fertilizer price increases and tobacco price declines, and sudden and sharp declines in capital inflows, including external aid. In recent years, Malawi has suffered from increasingly frequent weather shocks—as shown in figure 2.12, Malawi has faced five droughts since 1990 that affected more than 20 percent of the population. Weather shocks are invariably accompanied by declines in agricultural output and slowdowns in economic activity linked to agriculture.[6] This in turn leads to declines in government revenue that, accompanied by increased expenditure on

Figure 2.8 Inflation Rate in Malawi, 1980–2015

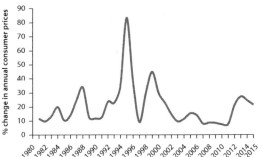

Sources: Estimates based on World Development Indicators data and Reserve Bank of Malawi data.

Figure 2.9 Real Interest Rate in Malawi, 1980–2014

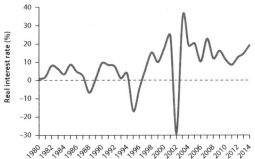

Sources: Estimates based on World Development Indicators data and Reserve Bank of Malawi data.

Figure 2.10 Real Exchange Rate in Malawi, 1980–2015

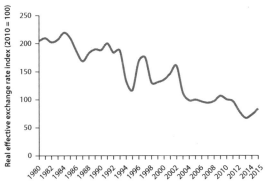

Sources: Estimates based on World Development Indicators data and Reserve Bank of Malawi data.

Figure 2.11 Fiscal Balances in Malawi, 1980–2015

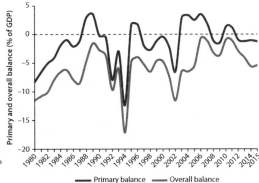

Sources: Estimates based on World Development Indicators data and Reserve Bank of Malawi data.

relief to the weather-affected poor, have in the past often destabilized government budgets. The most common response has been to delay adjustment and manage somehow while awaiting external aid.

However, as important as external shocks are in explaining instability, considerable evidence indicates that economic policies and management explain declines in growth in low- and middle-income countries much more than external shocks. Empirical research reported in Raddatz (2007) found that the emphasis on external shocks as a source of economic instability in low-income countries is probably misplaced. Although external shocks have an economically meaningful effect on real activity (especially relative to the average economic performance of low-income countries), they account for only a small fraction of the volatility of these countries' real GDP. The most important causes of economic instability appear to be internal and related to economic management.

Table 2.4 External Shocks and Policy-Induced Shocks Affecting Malawi's Economy, 1992–2015

Year(s)	Weather or global economic shock	External aid shock	Policy-induced shock	Overall fiscal balance (% of GDP including grants)	Inflation (year over year % change in CPI)	Interest rates (end of period, compounded 91 days Treasury bill)
1992	Severe drought in first quarter, 67% decline in maize output compared with previous year	Cutback in donor nonhumanitarian aid by 3.7% of GDP from earlier projections (asking for multiparty government)	Labor unrest due to low increase in minimum wage, average rise in wages and salaries >50% in the economy, monetary accommodation	Fiscal year 1992/93: –8.5	23.2	20.4
1994	Severe drought in 1993–94 crop season	—	Massive election-related budget overruns in all ministries in first quarter of fiscal year 1994/95; sizable unbudgeted expenditure, salaries raised, severe labor unrest; free primary education introduced, 12,000 new teachers hired, overspending financed by Reserve Bank of Malawi	Fiscal year 1993/94: –4.0 Fiscal year 1994/95: –11.4	34.7	40.6
1997–98	—	—	Spending overruns, teacher recruitment, slackened revenue performance; in fiscal year 1997/98, expenditure slippages led to spending of 4.25% of GDP in excess of program; 47% increase in civil service wages	Fiscal year 1997/98: –5.1	1997: 9.1 1998: 29.8	1997: 19.2 1998: 42.2
2001–03	Drought: maize output declined by a third in 2001; maize operation equivalent to 3% of GDP in fiscal year 2002/03 budget	External budgetary financing delayed due to policy slippages	Bad policy decision about sale of entire reserve stock; expenditure 3.5% above programmed amount in fiscal year 2000/01; parastatals bailout, augmented civil service wages, increase in low-priority spending such as travel and representation; during fiscal years 2002/03–2003/04, expenditure in excess of 5% of GDP over program; government domestic debt doubled during this period	Fiscal year 2000/01: –4.5 Fiscal year 2001/02: –5.6 Fiscal year 2002/03: –6.4 Fiscal year 2003/04: –4.3	2001: 27.4 2002: 14.7 2003: 9.6	2001: 45.7 2002: 36.1 2003: 33.1

table continues next page

Table 2.4 External Shocks and Policy-Induced Shocks Affecting Malawi's Economy, 1992–2015 (continued)

Year(s)	Weather or global economic shock	External aid shock	Policy-induced shock	Overall fiscal balance (% of GDP including grants)	Inflation (year over year % change in CPI)	Interest rates (end of period, compounded 91 days Treasury bill)
2008–09	Terms-of-trade shock: fertilizer bid prices almost 51% higher than budgeted	—	Elections in May 2009; loosened monetary and fiscal policies	Fiscal year 2008/09: −4.6	2008: 8.7 2009: 8.4	2008: 13.4 2009: 7.1
2010–12	—	Significant decline in donor grants in response to unsustainable policies: grants declined from 10.3% of GDP in fiscal year 2009/10 to 3.1% of GDP in fiscal year 2011/12	International Monetary Fund program off track, exchange rate policy misaligned; significant foreign exchange shortages	Fiscal year 2009/10: 0.2 Fiscal year 2010/11: −2.0 Fiscal year 2011/12: −4.9	2010: 7.4 2011: 7.6 2012: 21.3	2010: 6.2 2011: 7.7 2012: 20.0
2013–15	Heavy floods in 2015 followed by drought	Donor grants resumed in fiscal year 2012/13, but on-budget share declined significantly after "cashgate"	Theft of public funds discovered in second half of 2013; fiscal year 2014/slippages 2% of GDP; unplanned recruitment of 10,500 teachers, unbudgeted wage increase (1.25% of GDP)	Fiscal year 2013/14: −5.5 Fiscal year 2014/15: −5.7 Fiscal year 2015/16: −6.1	2013: 28.3 2014: 23.8 2015: 21.9	2013: 32.3 2014: 26.8 2015: 24.2

Source: International Monetary Fund, Article IV reports for various years during 1990–2015.
Note: — = not available. CPI = consumer price index; GDP = gross domestic product.

Figure 2.12 External Shocks in Malawi, 1979–2016

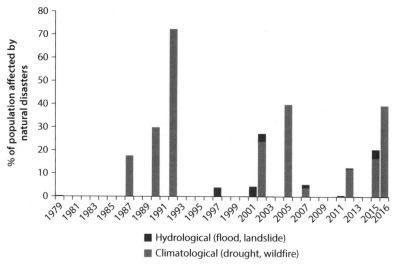

Source: Estimates based on data from the International Disaster Database.

Earlier, Bleaney (1996) also found that policy-induced macroeconomic instability is an important negative influence on investment and growth in low- and middle-income countries.[7]

Consistent with these findings, close examination of Malawi's economic history since 1990 suggests that economic management has been a bigger source of instability than external shocks. Table 2.4 summarizes seven episodes in the past 25 years during which Malawi faced significant macroeconomic instability.[8] In addition to external shocks, the table lists policy-induced shocks, that is, instances when inappropriate policy responses to external shocks or policy actions themselves pushed the economy to instability, evident in significant volatility in macroeconomic variables.

In almost all instances of external shocks, policy actions either exacerbated the impact of the shock or prolonged it. As a response to crises, the government has mostly adopted ad hoc expenditure cuts, postponed expenditures, and run arrears without making hard fiscal adjustments. Clearly, some of these measures hurt future growth or sowed the seeds for future crises by building up fiscal pressures. In contrast, when the fiscal situation was well managed during 2004–09, the economy survived the food crisis of 2005, the terms-of-trade shock in 2008, and the 2008–09 financial crisis without any instability (figure 2.13).

Moreover, several episodes of instability resulted from bad economic management with no external shock. The following were especially egregious instances of poor management: (a) in 1997–98, expenditure slippages led to spending of 4.25 percent of GDP in excess of programmed levels, and there were spending overruns across ministries, unbudgeted teacher recruitment, and a 47 percent

Figure 2.13 Terms of Trade in Malawi, 1980–2015

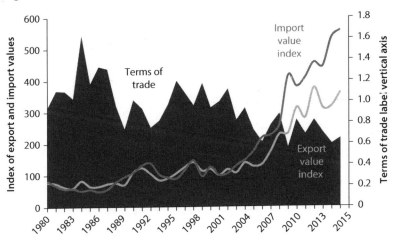

Source: Estimates based on World Development Indicator data.

increase in civil service wages; (b) the fixed exchange rate experiment during 2005–12 resulted in the buildup of large macroeconomic balances and led to instability when the peg was finally abandoned in 2012; and (c) the theft of public funds discovered in the second half of 2013 led major donors to suspend aid through on-budget means, disrupting financing of the fiscal year 2013/14 and 2014/15 budgets. Since 1990, there have been four instances in which external aid has declined abruptly. Aside from 1992, when donors withheld aid to apply pressure for the adoption of a multiparty system, in all other instances, aid was withheld due to loss of donor confidence in the government's ability to manage the economy.

The review of historical evidence identifies some recurring issues in Malawi's economic management during episodes of instability, including weak fiscal management, lack of fiscal space, and inappropriate policy interventions in agricultural markets, especially maize markets.[9] Of the three, weak fiscal management has been at the heart of most episodes of macroeconomic instability. Several aspects of weak fiscal management in Malawi deserve attention:

- *Weak medium-term budget planning.* Large, often unbudgeted, recruitments have derailed several budgets in the past. Similarly, regular public wage increases have been postponed and subsequently made in an unplanned and lumpy fashion, disrupting fiscal plans. Estimates of revenues and grants have been repeatedly over-optimistic and based on unrealistic growth assumptions.
- *Budget execution, perhaps most importantly budgetary indiscipline and weak expenditure control.* Preelection budget overruns have been routine. In addition, unproductive recurrent expenditures such as on travel, representation, and payroll irregularities have been built up repeatedly and then have had to be corrected. Recurring off-budget commitments and arrears have needed to be

normalized on multiple occasions. The inability to reduce corruption and the fraudulent use of public resources has also been a major challenge.

- *Slow fiscal response to shocks.* In most instances, response to weather shocks has been drawn out and slow. Generally, the government approach is to muddle through such situations. The government has responded to these crises mostly by adopting ad hoc expenditure cuts, postponing expenditures, and running arrears without making hard fiscal adjustments, thus sowing the seeds for future crises. At times, it is also an issue of incentives, with the government being in a game-like situation with donors and attempting to maximize the grants it can receive in times of crisis. While donors often ramp up grants in times of weather-related crises, these funds often take time to be mobilized, delaying adjustment.

- *Soft budget constraint.* Historically, the Reserve Bank of Malawi has financed excess government deficits whenever the need has arisen. This monetary accommodation of demand for fiscal resources takes the pressure off of the executive to stay within the prudent budgetary limits.

An exercise to "predict" Malawi's public debt-to-GDP ratio found evidence of weak fiscal management in that actual debt is much higher than predicted debt. The exercise "predicted" Malawi's public debt-to-GDP ratio from year to year based on 2007 as the starting year, when the Highly Indebted Poor Countries (HIPC) initiative and the Multilateral Debt Relief Initiative (MDRI) took effect, factoring in fiscal deficits, nominal GDP growth, and the impact of changes in the exchange rate on the foreign exchange component of public debt. It found that by 2015, actual debt was 18 percentage points of GDP higher than predicted debt; in other words, while predicted debt increased by just 10 percentage points of GDP between 2007 and 2015, actual debt increased by a much larger 28 percentage points. This implies either that debt increased as a result of factors not related to fiscal deficits and the impact of changes in the exchange rate on foreign exchange debt (such as bank recapitalization costs or borrowing by parastatals) or that fiscal deficits were underreported.

An additional structural issue is the lack of available policy buffers that would enable the government to respond more effectively to shocks. Lack of policy space to maneuver in the event of sudden external disturbances has left Malawi unable to implement the much-needed countervailing policies (World Bank 2015), contributing to higher volatility. Until 2006, when debt relief under the HIPC initiative and the MDRI took place, Malawi had a large debt-to-GDP ratio that limited its ability to borrow out of a fiscal crisis. In the short span of nine years after 2006, Malawi's debt sustainability is under pressure once again. Permanent fiscal adjustment is needed to create space for interventions when shocks hit, without waiting for aid to arrive. Given how critical fiscal management is to maintaining economic stability and growth, the following section delves into fiscal issues in greater detail.

The Challenges of Fiscal Management

Malawi's recent economic history has been one of significant volatility in fiscal outturns and performance. This has triggered knock-on effects, with fiscal indiscipline leading to large domestic borrowing requirements, crowding out private sector lending, and stoking nonfood inflation. Fiscal dominance has also undermined the effectiveness of monetary policy, leaving Malawi with the costs of a tight monetary policy (restraining credit growth) but without the benefits (falling inflation). The burden of financing such persistent fiscal deficits has also led to a growing share of public expenditure going toward servicing domestic debt, compressing the available space for service delivery and public investment.

In Malawi's current macroeconomic framework, fiscal outcomes affect growth through various channels. Fiscal deficits feed into debt, and high public indebtedness creates macroeconomic uncertainty about future inflation and taxes. Such uncertainty, combined with low credibility, increases real interest rates on the market portion of debt. Macroeconomic uncertainty also adversely affects the private sector investment climate and shortens horizons, leading to an emphasis on short-term business activity often associated mostly with trading. As a result, there are both high volatility in real interest rates on domestic debt, real exchange rates, and inflation rates and a preference for holding foreign exchange instead of local currency assets. In addition, a large share of interest payments in government spending crowds out growth-supporting public expenditure.

All of the benefits of HIPC and MDRI debt relief to Malawi dissipated within a decade. Thanks to significant debt relief under HIPC and MDRI, Malawi's external debt-to-GDP ratio fell from 88.7 in 2002 to 13.5 in 2006. This sharp reduction lowered macroeconomic uncertainty, and the improved outlook for debt sustainability helped to support the growth spurt that took place between 2003 and 2010. However, as mentioned, Malawi's public debt has grown rapidly since 2006, and the debt-to-GDP ratio more than doubled between 2007 and 2015. As shown in figure 2.14, Malawi's public debt dynamics have deteriorated significantly in recent years due to large primary deficits, and large gaps have developed between interest rates (external and domestic) and GDP growth, both in nominal and real terms. As a result, a high degree of macroeconomic uncertainty continues to surround the sustainability of Malawi's public debt.

In tackling public debt, one of Malawi's major fiscal challenges is the high level of government expenditure related to resources. Malawi's public sector expenditures are relatively high, at more than 35 percent of GDP. Expenditures relative to GDP and relative to revenues and grants have grown over the years as the government has taken on increasingly large expenditures for human development and agricultural subsidies (figure 2.15).

This high level of government expenditure without commensurate benefits places a heavy burden on the private sector. The high level of government consumption in excess of domestic resources is financed by domestic borrowing, aid, and implicit sources of public finance such as seigniorage. Over the

Figure 2.14 Level of Debt in Malawi, 2004–2018

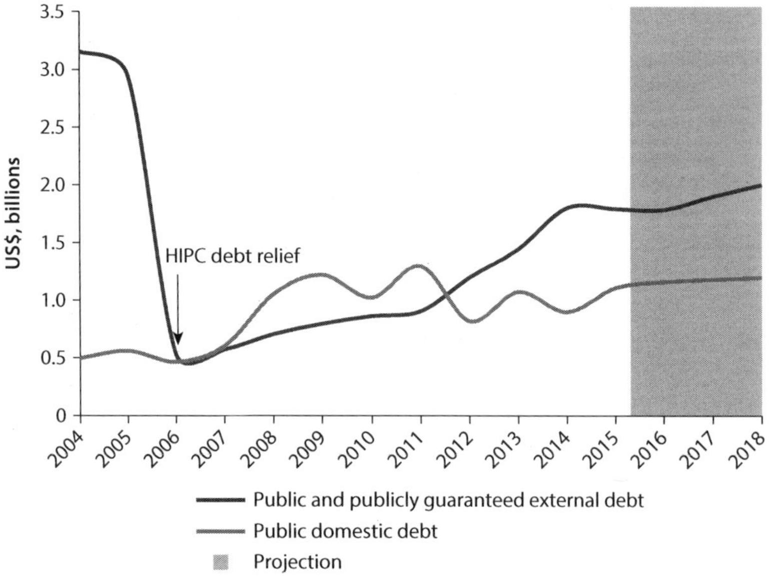

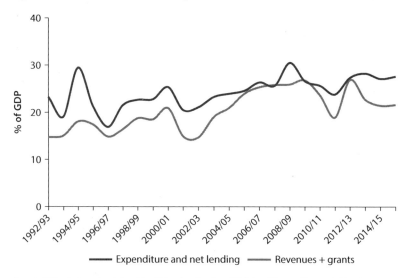

Source: Estimates based on the debt sustainability analysis conducted for this book.
Note: HIPC = Highly Indebted Poor Countries initiative.

Figure 2.15 Ratio of Government Expenditures to GDP in Malawi, 1992–2015

Sources: Estimates based on International Monetary Fund and Ministry of Finance, Economic Planning, and Development data.
Note: GDP = gross domestic product.

years, seigniorage and inflation have placed a heavy burden on the private sector. As discussed in Le and Kandoole (2016), Malawi's tax collection is high given the country's stage of development and relative to its tax potential or taxable capacity (figure 2.16). Doing business in Malawi is therefore expensive in terms of both tax burden and compliance costs, and the tax burden on factors of production is also high.

Not only is expenditure high, but those resources are also not necessarily used in the most efficient or effective way. While Malawi has achieved significant improvements in health outcomes, less can be said about the use of resources for educational and agricultural subsidies (Favaro 2015). As discussed in chapter 3, agricultural subsidies have resulted in large expenditures on imported fertilizer, exposing the country's external position to bigger risks without any commensurate macroeconomic or even microeconomic gains.

A related challenge has been the degree of "elite capture" of major public expenditure programs, which often reduces the effectiveness of public spending and makes reforming the use of expenditures more difficult. Elite capture includes recurring pressures to grow both the size of the public sector and the level of public sector compensation as well as the very high costs of civil service retrenchment, along with the high costs of nonwage benefits, allowances, and travel (especially at senior grades). In addition, public procurement in major programs such as fertilizer as well as in goods and services contracts and infrastructure has been a major challenge and the source of several grand corruption cases in recent years.

Figure 2.16 Tax Collection Relative to GDP per Capita in Malawi

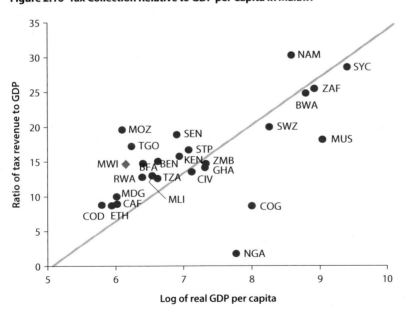

Source: Estimates based on World Development Indicators data.
Note: GDP = gross domestic product.

From Falling Behind to Catching Up • http://dx.doi.org/10.1596/978-1-4648-1194-4

Figure 2.17 Role of Donor Grants in Malawi, 1992–2015

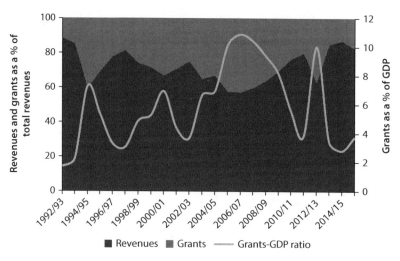

Sources: Estimates based on International Monetary Fund and Ministry of Finance, Economic Planning, and Development data.
Note: GDP = gross domestic product.

Malawi's high dependence on aid has negative implications for governance. Malawi has been among the top receivers of official development assistance (ODA) in low- and middle-income Sub-Saharan Africa, averaging US$60 per capita over the past seven years—or around US$1 billion annually (Le and Kandoole 2016)—compared with an average of around US$50 for the Sub-Saharan African region. Although the share of ODA channeled through the budget has declined significantly while domestic resource mobilization has increased, the role of external aid remains prominent, with grants totaling around 2.8 percent of GDP in fiscal years 2014/15 (figure 2.17). Since the "cashgate" scandal, an increasing share of ODA has been disbursed outside of government systems (70 percent in fiscal year 2015/16, compared with 30 percent in fiscal year 2008/09) (World Bank 2016). Heavy aid dependence can come with costs, including uncertainty and weak accountability of the government.

Notes

1. Malawi, Zambia, and Zimbabwe.

2. For more discussion and analysis of these periods, see Kandoole, Stylianou, and von Carnap (2016).

3. Sub-Saharan Africa excluding Malawi is a heterogeneous group that includes several resource-rich countries, including a few middle-income countries with economies very different from that of Malawi. Therefore, as described in Kandoole, Stylianou, and von Carnap (2016), a few Sub-Saharan African countries were selected that were Malawi's peers in 2015 because they were low-income countries with agricultural value added above 20 percent of GDP, in addition to being nonfragile states.

The peers were also non-resource-rich for most of the period under investigation (1990–2015), although some have become resource-rich in recent years (Burkina Faso, Mozambique, Niger).

4. This approach essentially looks at output (and hence income) as a product of labor and physical capital. Therefore, accounts are created that account for labor and physical capital growth. TFP refers to residual growth that remains unaccounted for and is thought of as growth due to factors that reflect the organization of economic activity.

5. To account for increasing schooling and returns to education, the human capital index was included in the decomposition analysis using the augmented production function approach. Having removed the human capital effect, TFP became a better measure of productivity growth.

6. For example, simultaneous floods and drought in 2015 caused a 30.2 percent reduction in national output of maize, leaving 2.8 million Malawians food-insecure and dependent on relief. As a consequence, the country registered GDP growth of just 2.8 percent in 2015 (Kandoole, Stylianou, and von Carnap 2016). This was followed by a deeper drought in 2016, leaving 6.7 million Malawians food-insecure and resulting in even lower GDP growth of 2.5 percent. Malawi's terms of trade have also been volatile, although there have been few large abrupt shifts.

7. The argument is that "poor macroeconomic management creates uncertainty about relative prices and the absolute price level which discourages investment; it is also possible that poor macroeconomic management inhibits growth of TFP more directly, for example by inhibiting risk-taking and resource transfer between sectors." Empirical research also shows that the impact of external shocks on growth is mostly through a reduction of the growth residual (TFP) rather than the rate of investment (Guillaumont, Guillaumont-Jeanneney, and Brun 1999).

8. 1990 was selected rather arbitrarily. Similar episodes also took place in the 1980s.

9. Government interventions in the maize market have often had a destabilizing effect in the past, as noted in table 2.4. This is discussed further in chapter 3.

References

Bleaney, M. F. 1996. "Macroeconomic Stability, Investment, and Growth in Developing Countries." *Journal of Development Economics* 48 (2): 461–77.

Dabalen, A., A. de la Fuente, A. Goyal, W. Karamba, N. Viet Nguyen, and T. Tanaka. 2017. *Pathways to Prosperity in Rural Malawi*. Directions in Development. Washington, DC: World Bank.

Dollar, D., and A. Kraay. 2002. "Growth Is Good for the Poor." *Journal of Economic Growth* 7 (3): 195–225.

Easterly, W., and S. Fischer. 2001. "Inflation and the Poor." Policy Research Working Paper 2335, World Bank, Washington, DC.

Enache, M., E. Ghani, and S. O'Connell. 2016. "Structural Transformation in Africa and Malawi: A Historical View." Malawi Country Economic Memorandum background paper, World Bank, Washington, DC.

Favaro, E. 2015. "Government Expenditure, Aid, and Economic Growth." Malawi Policy Note, Macroeconomics and Fiscal Management Global Practice, World Bank, Lilongwe.

Go, D. S., and J. Page. 2008. "Africa at a Turning Point? Growth, Aid, and External Shocks." Africa Development Essay, World Bank, Washington, DC.

Guillaumont, P., S. Guillaumont-Jeanneney, and J. F. Brun. 1999. "How Instability Lowers African Growth." *Journal of African Economies* 8 (1): 87–107.

Hausmann, R., D. Rodrik, and A. Velasco. 2005. "Growth Diagnostics." John F. Kennedy School of Government, Harvard University, Cambridge, MA.

Kandoole, P., E. Stylianou, and T. von Carnap. 2016. "Malawi's Growth Performance in a Historical Perspective: Implications for Future Growth Strategy." Malawi Country Economic Memorandum background paper, World Bank, Washington, DC.

Le, T. M., and P. Kandoole. 2016. "Malawi's Tax System: Issues and the Way Ahead." Malawi Country Economic Memorandum background paper, World Bank, Washington, DC.

NSO (National Statistical Office). 2014. *Malawi Labor Force Survey 2013.* Zomba: Government of Malawi.

Raddatz, C. 2007. "Are External Shocks Responsible for the Instability of Output in Low-Income Countries?" *Journal of Development Economics* 84 (1): 155–87.

World Bank. 2001. *World Development Report 2000/2001: Attacking Poverty.* New York: Oxford University Press.

———. 2015. *Feet on the Ground, Eyes on the Horizon: Assessing Vulnerability and Resilience in SSA.* Washington, DC: World Bank.

———. 2016. *Malawi Economic Monitor: Absorbing Shocks, Building Resilience.* Macroeconomics and Fiscal Management Global Practice. Washington, DC: World Bank.

CHAPTER 3

The Critical Role of Agriculture in Growth and Poverty Reduction

The agriculture sector remains of central importance for Malawi to achieve its development objectives and fight poverty. While the significance of agriculture in Malawi's economy has dropped over the past 50 years, from providing half to providing less than one-third of total gross domestic product (GDP) by 2015, Malawi's economy remains among the world's 15 national economies most dependent on agriculture (Benson and Edelman 2016). The agriculture sector also plays a key role in poverty reduction, as poverty in Malawi is still mainly a rural phenomenon and is closely linked to agriculture.[1] Around 87 percent of Malawi's households are engaged in agriculture to at least some degree, and the sector provides employment for 64 percent of the population. However, the productivity of the agriculture sector remains relatively low, largely because most of the sector operates on the basis of just one rain-fed crop per year.

The agriculture sector is also critically important to the food security of households and the nation as a whole. As discussed in Benson and Edelman (2016), food security for households depends to a large extent on own production of food. With most crops being rain-fed, there is considerable year-to-year variability in production and consequently in the food security of households across the country. Analysis of data from the third Integrated Household Survey found that an estimated 32.5 percent of households in Malawi have "very low food security" (NSO 2012). Faced with food shortages, households resort to coping strategies such as depleting their savings, selling their assets, and changing their food consumption patterns, which can adversely affect household welfare and lead to poor nutritional outcomes.

In order to achieve meaningful contributions to human and economic development, strategies for the country as a whole thus have to address the key constraints to growth in the agriculture sector. This chapter describes these constraints for different crops or actors and lays out key issues for agricultural policy in Malawi. It begins with an overview of challenges in the agriculture sector, looking at both smallholder production and larger operations. It then reviews current government policies aimed at supporting the sector and assesses their impacts, providing a basis for future policy directions.

Moreover, while it is clear that Malawi's agriculture sector needs deep investment in order to boost resilience and productivity, the critical binding constraints to development are mostly related to policy choices. These constraints include the legacy of past interventions, with regard to both how Malawi's key agriculture sector institutions function despite numerous attempts at reform and the enduring policy restrictions that dampen incentives toward greater commercialization.

Lack of Change in the Agriculture Sector

For both smallholder farmers and larger commercially oriented operations, the level of crop diversification remains low. Both smallholders and larger commercial farmers focus on small groups of crops, although their respective composition differs. Smallholders are predominantly engaged in the farming of maize, tobacco, and vegetables. In particular, the vast majority of households (94 percent) are engaged in the production of maize, the staple of the diet of most Malawians. Commercial estate farming is mostly limited to the export crops of sugar, tea, and coffee. Given the small domestic market and a nonconducive business and policy environment, private companies have found it unattractive to produce for local and export markets or to enter into lower-value crops other than the few currently produced for export.

Agricultural (and particularly maize) markets in Malawi are characterized by a low level of market connectivity. As shown in table 3.1, rice and tobacco are the only crops grown primarily for sale, with 58 and 96 percent of producers, respectively, reportedly selling them. The percentages are much lower for groundnuts (36 percent) and pigeon peas (27 percent) and lowest for maize (14 percent). While this pattern is often rational at the individual level, it perpetuates a cycle

Table 3.1 Share of Agricultural Crops That Are Sold in Malawi
% of farming households

Crop	Produce	Of those producing, those who reported any sales	Of those selling, mean portion of harvest sold
Maize	93.6	13.9	35.1
Local varieties	52.5	10.9	32.1
Hybrids, recycled hybrids, or improved open-pollinated varieties	52.8	16.8	37.1
Groundnuts	25.9	36.1	45.4
Pigeon peas	20.7	26.5	53.9
Beans	8.6	20.7	48.0
Rice	4.7	58.3	49.3
Tobacco	14.4	95.5	86.8

Source: Benson and Edelman 2016.

of thin agricultural markets and food insecurity. Farmers are hesitant to engage in trade because they face high transaction costs (particularly from transportation) and high risk of transaction failure since traders may not be around when the produce is ready to be sold. Similarly, traders cannot be sure whether there will be enough suppliers in a given market to justify the high costs of getting there. As a result, few maize farmers can profit from seasonally high demand for their produce, and trade is less effective in reducing price differentials both within the country and over time.

Maize production and, in turn, prices remain highly volatile. Despite a relatively favorable agroecological environment and large government subsidies, maize price volatility in Malawi is the highest in the region, with the exception of Harare (figure 3.1). Price increases between May and February amount to around 60 percent on average, inviting hoarding and speculative behavior even by relatively well-off individuals otherwise not engaged in trading activities. While weather shocks have a major influence on maize production, their impacts and other external effects on prices could be better managed and largely mitigated, as discussed later.

The low level of crop diversification exposes smallholders to significant market risk, particularly in the case of tobacco. Aside from maize, smallholders' livelihoods continue to depend on tobacco receipts. This dependence exposes them to large risks with respect to swings in global demand, as seen in the 2016 marketing season, when a combination of shrinking Chinese demand, shortage of foreign exchange of key trading partners, and concerns about crop quality led to relatively low sales prices. Such difficulties reflect a general trend of decreasing prices and a slowdown in demand for tobacco globally, resulting in a decline in

Figure 3.1 Maize Price Volatility in Malawi and Elsewhere in Sub-Saharan Africa, 2004–15

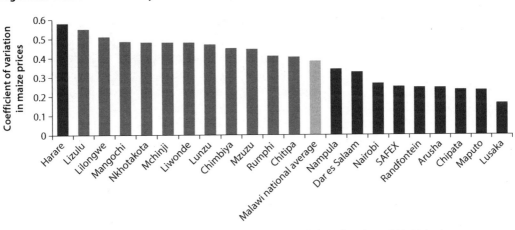

■ Selected markets outside of Malawi ■ Selected markets within Malawi

Source: Benson and Edelman 2016, based on statistics reported by market information systems or statistical offices of Kenya, Malawi, Mozambique, South Africa, Tanzania, and Zambia as well as by the Famine Early Warning System Network in Zimbabwe.
Note: SAFEX = South African Futures Exchange.

demand for Malawi's tobacco crop of about 1 percent each year on average. While an increased focus on quality might help to strengthen Malawi's position in the world market in the short term, it seems doubtful whether tobacco can continue to be the main source of income for both farmers and the country as a whole for long.

Various environmental risks also affect agricultural production as soil fertility continues to decline. Conservative estimates suggest that Malawi lost an average of 4 percent of the value of its annual agricultural production between 1980 and 2012 due mostly to droughts, floods, pests, diseases, and other factors (Giertz and others 2015). This figure does not take into account postharvest losses (for example, from inadequate storage or price fluctuations) and masks catastrophic household-level impacts in the particularly affected regions during specific years. The bulk of the losses stem from the staples of maize (30 percent, mostly in the central region and around Blantyre) and cassava (26 percent, around Blantyre and Mzuzu), reflecting their large share of smallholder production. In addition, lack of diversification and crop rotation, together with land pressures resulting in deforestation and increased use of marginal land, have gradually yet persistently depleted nutrients in Malawi's soils. Without changed practices, greater and greater volumes of chemical fertilizer are required to prevent Malawi's already low yields from falling even further.

Recurring droughts present the largest risk and have recently increased in frequency, but few measures have been undertaken to mitigate this risk. While local differences may be large and precise impacts are nearly impossible to predict, dry spells seem to follow a pattern and are often related to the El Niño weather phenomenon, which brings drought conditions across Southern Africa. Such global weather patterns are often foreseeable long before their consequences materialize on the ground. Malawi could therefore benefit from taking a longer-term view of food security and building up reserves before disaster strikes.[2] Notably, although more drought-tolerant crop varieties are often available, their take-up is low due to factors such as harvest seasons that overlap with other crops, limited access to finance, or simply lack of knowledge. Coverage of irrigation also remains low, despite substantial investments in engineered irrigation schemes for large-scale commercial purposes as well as smallholders. Less than 3 percent of agricultural areas in Malawi were under engineered irrigation in 2015. Most crops are not profitable enough to cover the costs of operating and maintaining irrigation infrastructure, including maize and other staple foods given current price levels, at least when grown on a small scale.

Ineffective Efforts to Support the Agriculture Sector

As the main staple food, maize assumes a key role in government programs for national food security. The focus on maize is evident in the size of the Farm Input Subsidy Program (FISP), which peaked at US$126.5 million (75 percent of the budget for agriculture or 3 percent of GDP) in fiscal year 2014/15 (World Bank 2015), although the program has been scaled down significantly since then to around 1 percent of GDP in the fiscal year 2016/17 budget. FISP, initially envisaged as an agricultural productivity-enhancing program, has the stated objective of providing subsidies to resource-poor smallholder farmers. In addition to FISP, the government regularly makes payments to the Agricultural Development and Marketing Corporation (ADMARC) in order to subsidize prices and make up for inefficiencies in their marketing of maize.

Although maize production has risen since the inception of FISP in fiscal year 2005/06, yield targets are still far from being met, and food security for the poor has not improved. Production per capita rose on average between 2006 and 2009 but then stalled after 2010 due to the adverse effects of drought and flooding as well as less efficient implementation of FISP. Despite average yields having risen from 1 to 1.8 metric tons per hectare through FISP, they are still well short of the proclaimed yields of 7.1 metric tons per hectare. Furthermore, increased maize production has not contributed to higher consumption levels among the ultra-poor. Around 24.5 percent of the population was below the food poverty line in fiscal year 2010/11, compared with 22.4 percent six years earlier. The share of population vulnerable to hunger fell from 20.2 percent on average between 2003 and 2006 to 3 percent between 2007 and 2012 but then rose again to 17.5 percent during 2013–17 (Benson and Edelman 2016; MVAC 2016).

Although FISP aims to provide subsidies to resource-poor smallholder farmers, targeting and efficiency have been problematic. Before the recent adoption of a coupon model, the program included large public sector procurement contracts for fertilizer supply, resulting in rent seeking and elite capture. Furthermore, data from the Integrated Household Panel Survey shows that a larger share of subsidized inputs benefits the better-off and relatively resource-rich parts of the population, with 37 percent of households in the bottom three consumption deciles receiving inputs under the FISP versus 53 percent in the top three deciles.[3] Moreover, there is strong evidence that poorer farmers sell the vouchers instead of redeeming them for inputs. In such cases, the program functions in effect as a highly inefficient cash transfer to the extreme poor and to relatively unproductive farmers. For more productive farmers, the subsidy—in combination with a maize export ban and limited access to storage—drives down producer prices. In addition to discouraging farmers who would like to engage in maize production on a more commercial basis (which explains the low level of commercial maize production in Malawi), these policies might actually hurt farmers who have to sell their produce early in the season.

The government's large expenditures on FISP and other programs not only are costly but also do not provide the support necessary to advance the process of agricultural transformation. The target of food self-sufficiency through increased maize production comes at a high cost to government, and its sustainability seems doubtful in the face of rising population pressure and quickly degrading soils, which require the ever-increasing use of costly inputs such as fertilizer. While raising output in the short run, the increased use of fertilizer and improved seeds does little to restore soil fertility or sustainably improve farmers' resilience unless complementary measures are taken. The large government expenses therefore cannot be seen as much-needed investment in agriculture but rather as a form of consumption that only improves income in one year, before requiring renewed (and even greater) support in the next one. Furthermore, market interventions such as price controls and export restrictions have created disincentives for farmers to invest in their maize production to improve yields. The focus of government policy on maize also undermines efforts to diversify agricultural production toward other crops, which at the farm level might allow for greater resilience and improved soil conservation.

Moreover, closer analysis of regional price patterns reveals that the high volatility in maize prices is caused in large part by nontransparent market behavior by public sector institutions. Only 40 percent of the overall variability in maize prices in Malawi can be attributed to predictable and quantifiable seasonal factors (Benson and Edelman 2016), with much of the rest being due to nontransparent intervention strategies by ADMARC and the National Food Reserve Agency (NFRA), both parastatals under the Ministry of Agriculture, Irrigation, and Water Development. As the biggest buyer and seller in the market, ADMARC drives prices in both the procurement and selling seasons. ADMARC and NFRA have often failed to procure maize directly from farmers at harvest time when it is cheapest to do so and instead have bought from private traders later in the season, thus contributing to higher prices. Sales at subsidized prices later in the season then often create the need for the government to support ADMARC, as procurement prices have been unnecessarily high. Large commercial traders can speculate on when and at what prices ADMARC will intervene and adjust their actions accordingly, preventing smooth price development over the year (Giertz and others 2015).

Political interference and nontransparent market behavior by ADMARC also impede the functioning of the market. This situation creates a lot of room for speculation and hoarding as well as collusion between ADMARC officials and traders. A telling example is the pronounced decrease in maize prices relative to the regional reference—the South African Futures Exchange (SAFEX)—in the months before the 2014 presidential elections, when ADMARC received increased government funding to ramp up sales of subsidized maize (Benson and Edelman 2016).

Similarly, recurrent trade restrictions invite speculative behavior and complicate commercial operations. Under the banner of maintaining food security and keeping domestic prices low, Malawi has frequently resorted to export bans.[4] While bans have often been put in place following a relatively bad harvest, Malawi has been slow to rescind them during better ones, thus depriving both small-scale and commercial growers of potentially profitable export opportunities that could raise incomes and revenues. Furthermore, restrictions on private trading of maize during times of hunger likely contribute to continued price increases, as otherwise profitable trading across borders ceases. Other regulations and controls hamper the development of small-scale private trading of maize, which would help to deepen agricultural markets. For a small economy such as Malawi's, better integration with regional markets could help to reduce food price volatility. More competition would also help to reduce the hoarding of the few active traders, as potential for collusion is lower and traders would rather sell early to secure their market share. A recurring argument for maintaining export restrictions has been to ensure that any price impact of FISP should benefit only Malawian consumers rather than being exported. However, under the current system, a small number of politically connected large traders have seemingly profited the most from this producer support.

Finally, in the face of growing population pressure and limited natural resources, pressure on Malawi's agriculture sector will continue to increase. Like many countries in Sub-Saharan Africa, Malawi has experienced a rapid drop in mortality but persistently high fertility. The country is experiencing an annual population growth rate of more than 3.0 percent, which implies that the population is doubling every 23 years. As such, the demographic transition remains sluggish (that is, the transition from high birth and death rates to low birth and death rates), running the risk of undermining Malawi's growth prospects.

Continued structural transformation will be critical, in particular toward more productive manufacturing and services sectors, which will include the movement of households from rural to urban areas. This transformation happens best on the basis of improved agricultural productivity and well-functioning agricultural markets that generate incomes, release agricultural labor, and stimulate demand in other sectors. Thus, progress on both fronts is equally important. Chapter 4 discusses factors that can help to facilitate such a transformation and stimulate private sector development and job creation in Malawi.

Notes

1. As mentioned in chapter 2, rural poverty has been estimated at 56.6 percent of the population and the urban poverty rate at 17.3 percent (NSO 2012).

2. These reserves can be financial as well as physical. In most years, options on SAFEX also have potential.

3. If this situation reflects a focus on food security through increased production across the social spectrum, then it is debatable why a substantial share of both poor (30 percent) and nonpoor households (42 percent) holding less than 0.3 hectare of land should also benefit, as these households would be expected to contribute only marginally to increased production (Dabalen and others 2017).

4. Export bans have been in place during 2005–07, 2008–09, and from 2012 onward (Benson and Edelman 2016). This definition includes both outright bans as well as the imposition of compulsory licensing schemes.

References

Benson, T., and B. Edelman. 2016. "Policies for Accelerating Growth in Agriculture and Agribusiness in Malawi." Malawi Country Economic Memorandum background paper, World Bank, Washington, DC.

Dabalen, A., A. de la Fuente, A. Goyal, W. Karamba, N. Viet Nguyen, and T. Tanaka. 2017. *Pathways to Prosperity in Rural Malawi*. Directions in Development. Washington, DC: World Bank.

Giertz, Å., J. Caballero, M. Dileva, D. Galperin, and T. Johnson. 2015. "Managing Agricultural Risk for Growth and Food Security in Malawi." Agricultural Global Practice Note 15, World Bank, Washington, DC.

MVAC (Malawi Vulnerability Assessment Committee). 2016. "National Food and Nutrition Security Forecast: April 2016 to March 2017." Government of Malawi, Lilongwe.

NSO (National Statistical Office). 2012. *Integrated Household Survey 2010–2011 (IHS-3)*. Zomba: Government of Malawi.

World Bank. 2015. *Malawi Economic Monitor: Managing Fiscal Pressures*. Macroeconomics and Fiscal Management Global Practice. Washington, DC: World Bank.

CHAPTER 4

The Need for Private Sector Investment and Job Creation for Future Growth

While transformation of the agriculture sector remains a critical development priority, it needs to go hand in hand with private sector growth and job creation, both key determinants of future growth and poverty reduction for Malawi. The country appears to be trapped in a cycle of low human capital and prevalence of capital-intensive industries, preventing the development of labor-intensive, income-generating, and poverty-alleviating sectors. In the future, Malawi's ability to achieve robust and sustainable growth will depend to a large extent on developing a thriving private sector, given that private enterprises play a key role in the economy as providers of goods and services, as importers and exporters, and as employers and taxpayers. Private sector development will also be critical for ensuring productive employment opportunities for Malawi's growing population, which are important not only for boosting overall economic growth but also for reducing poverty at the household level.

Although not insignificant efforts have been made to improve Malawi's business environment, costs remain high relative to comparator economies at similar levels of development. Significant aspects of the business environment remain characterized by a lack of transparency and predictability for investors. When added to the challenges of continued macroeconomic instability as well as major infrastructure deficits, the result is a private sector that is attempting mostly to preserve the value of existing investments rather than undertaking significant new investment.

Several constraints to private sector development and job creation have to be addressed to put Malawi on a higher development trajectory. This chapter identifies these constraints, first focusing on the factors that have affected private sector development. The analysis uses findings from recent Enterprise Surveys to understand better the relative importance of these constraints from the firms' perspective. The chapter then turns to some of the potential drivers of employment growth and identifies the constraints to job creation on both the supply and demand sides.

A Multitude of Constraints to Private Sector Development

The business structure in Malawi has been characterized as having a "missing middle." At one end of the spectrum is a sizable group of larger firms, usually found in agricultural processing as well as trading and retail. Malawi's economy is dominated by a very small number of large firms: in 2012, the five largest business enterprises accounted for 62 percent of total exports, while the 20 largest business enterprises accounted for 81 percent. At the other end of the spectrum is a vast number of households and microenterprises engaged in sales and small-scale manufacturing. In aggregate terms, the vast majority of exporters are small, with more than 65 percent of firms exporting goods at a value of less than US$50,000 per year.

The absence of mid-size firms in Malawi indicates that systemic constraints are holding back private sector development. While business cycles and swings in global demand affect enterprises in the short term, systemic constraints can hold back enterprise development over the longer run. The absence of a larger group of mid-size companies hints at a difficult business environment that constrains growth opportunities for small-size companies and favors firms with long-established networks. It also hints at the importance of insider relationships and the government's large share of demand for goods and services, which tends to favor established operators. The policy environment in Malawi is biased toward larger firms, partly due to the enduring legacy of heavy state intervention, further exacerbating the limited entry and success rate of new companies that would contribute to the diversification of exports and of the economy (Hoppe and Newfarmer 2014). In addition, the unstable macroeconomic environment and regulatory deficiencies affecting private sector activity similarly favor established firms with broad networks, enabling them to mitigate the many risks to business. Those issues notwithstanding, these findings underscore the potential inherent in structural transformation toward a more diversified economy beyond agriculture, as the few formally operating manufacturing firms are generally profitable.

Various factors constrain the earnings and employment potential of the formal private sector. The World Bank's *Doing Business Report 2016* ranks Malawi 141 out of 189 countries (the lowest among its neighbors) for the ease of establishing and running a business (World Bank 2015). In two nationally representative Enterprise Surveys conducted in 2009 (World Bank 2010) and 2014 (World Bank 2014), access to finance, reliability of electricity and water supply, and corruption consistently emerged as the top concerns (figure 4.1). Due to the challenging business environment, manufacturing firms in Malawi reportedly realize only 68 percent of the output they would be capable of

Figure 4.1 Obstacles to Conducting Private Business in Malawi and in Sub-Saharan Africa, by Size of Firm, Various Years

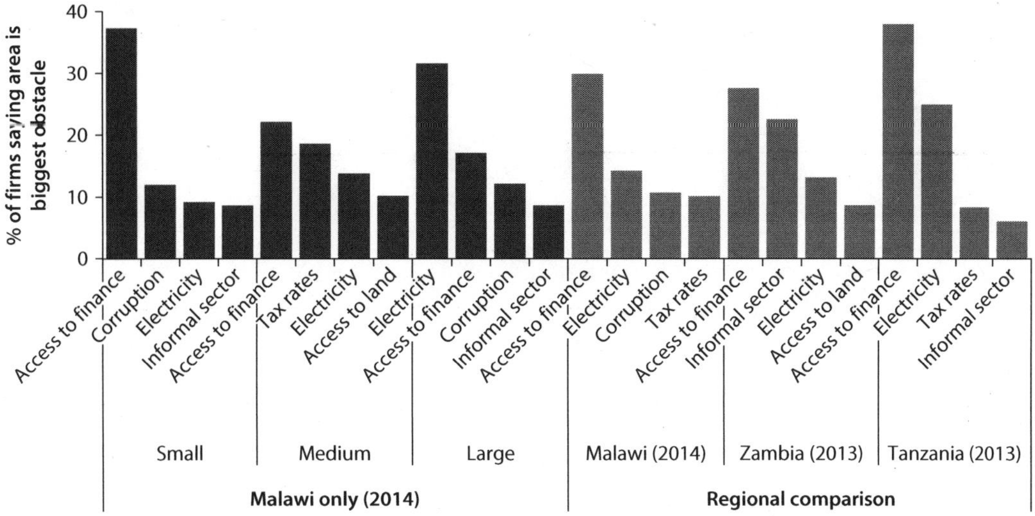

Source: Record, Hemphill, and Chilima 2016.

producing given their equipment and manpower, a share equal to that for Zambia but far less than for firms in Tanzania (82 percent).

As elsewhere in the region, the main obstacle is access to finance, especially for small- and medium-size firms. High interest rates, collateral requirements, and complex application procedures were cited as the main reasons for not taking up a loan. While 79 percent of large firms (more than 100 employees) had taken on credit in the year before the Enterprise Survey, only 63 percent of firms with 10–49 employees and 33 percent of firms with less than 5 employees had done so. These smaller firms mostly source their working capital from within their business, or owners give their private assets as collateral when taking up credit. Notably, economic research has shown that financing obstacles, particularly high interest rates, are more binding than other growth constraints (Ayyagari, Demirgüç-Kunt, and Maksimovic 2008). Since the end of 2012, nominal lending rates in Malawi have surged above the 90th percentile of the world distribution, comparing poorly against key country comparators as well as the Sub-Saharan African region and low-income benchmark countries (figure 4.2). The spread between deposit and lending rates has also widened (figure 4.3).

Recent analysis of Malawi's banking sector has found that high lending rates are driven primarily by macroeconomic factors, mostly inflation (Kibuuka and Vicente 2016). Inflation has been stubbornly high in Malawi since mid-2012, averaging more than 20 percent. High inflation lowers real incomes, so banks raise their lending rates to avoid a decline in their revenues. Persistently high inflation also increases economic uncertainty, raising banks' credit risk.

Figure 4.2 Nominal Lending Rates in Malawi and Comparator Countries, 2004–16

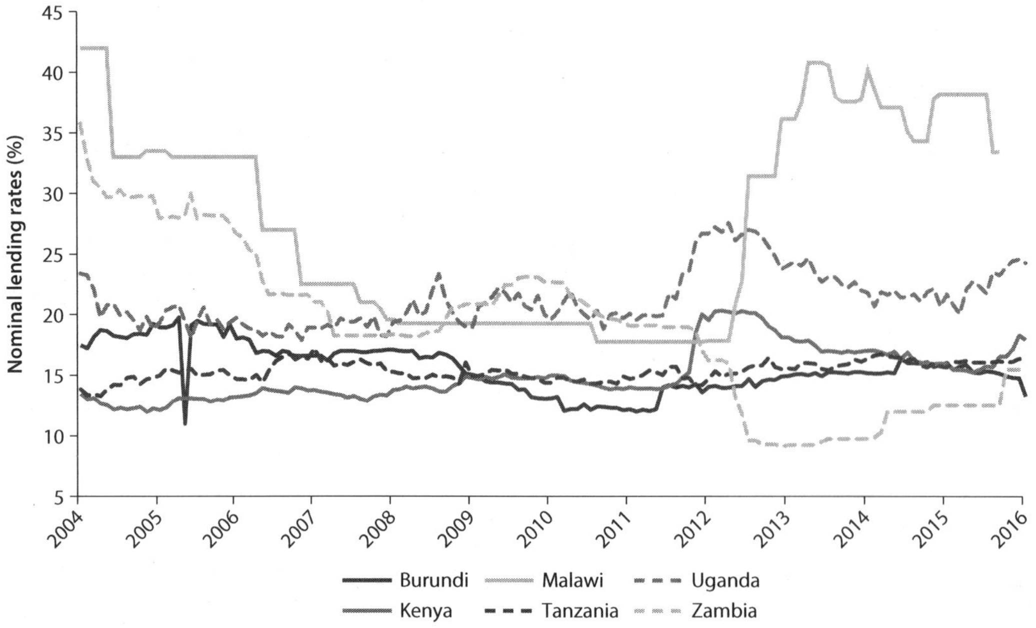

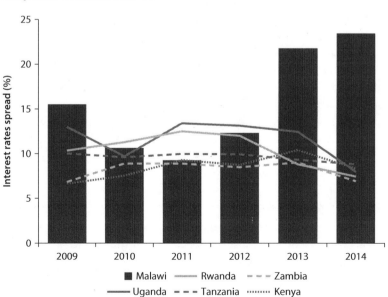

Source: Kibuuka and Vicente 2016.

Figure 4.3 Spread between Deposit and Lending Rates in Malawi and Comparator Countries, 2009–14

Source: Kibuuka and Vicente 2016.

From Falling Behind to Catching Up • http://dx.doi.org/10.1596/978-1-4648-1194-4

Electricity and water shortages also impose high costs on firms, with the situation seeming to have worsened since 2008. Firms of all sizes identified this as the second-biggest constraint to doing business in Malawi. On average, firms reported losing 5.1 percent of their annual sales due to electricity outages, with 40.9 percent of firms owning a backup generator. These utility problems affect larger enterprises the most, especially in the manufacturing sector. Operating backup generating facilities can triple the marginal cost of electricity supply for the private sector, undermining competitiveness; backup generators are only feasible in areas of business activity where margins can absorb such incremental costs.

Lack of investment in new generating capacity has resulted in a widening gap between Malawi's demand for energy and installed capacity. The total installed generating capacity of 365 megawatts (of which 98 percent is from hydropower sources along the Shire River) falls well short of estimated demand at around 440 megawatts. Climate variability and drought have had a significant impact on the availability of hydropower supply, leading to prolonged load shedding. Only 9 percent of the population has access to electricity.

Corruption is increasingly seen as a challenge to business activity. As shown in figure 4.1, corruption stands out as a more significant issue in Malawi than in neighboring Tanzania and Zambia, where corruption was not identified as one of the top obstacles. In Malawi, the percentage of companies that reported having been asked for bribes by public officials over the last year rose from 13.7 percent in 2008 to 24.0 percent in 2014. Overall, one in five interactions with the public sector was reported to have involved bribes, with the highest incidence being for construction permits, import licenses, and electricity connections—three areas that are likely to be key factors for successful business entry.

Another constraint to growth of Malawi's private sector is the high cost of domestic and international trade. Malawi has historically served as one of the more famous examples of a landlocked and small economy that suffers from high trade costs (Ksoll and Kunaka 2016). Previous studies have attributed these high costs to the long distance to seaports for overseas trade, the large gap between import and export volumes, an overreliance on road transport, competition on some trade routes (especially those through Mozambique), and delays in clearing cargo at border crossing points and at ports in neighboring Mozambique and Tanzania. Taken together, previous studies have established that high trade costs make it difficult for Malawian firms to gain access to low-cost imported inputs and to take advantage of export opportunities, including within the region. Given low income levels and a relatively modest population size, Malawi's domestic market provides limited opportunities—particularly in sectors where economies of scale are only possible if international markets are accessible.

Malawi's trade volumes are relatively small and highly imbalanced between imports and exports, which drives up trade costs. Despite impressive growth in the volume of Malawi's trade, trade remains small by international standards at around 3 million tons a year. Trade is highly imbalanced between imports and exports, and this imbalance is exacerbated by Malawi's narrow basket of products, as discussed in chapter 3. Most products traded undergo seasonal fluctuations, so large volumes are traded during the harvest season with moderate volumes throughout the remaining months (figure 4.4). Seasonal demand for transport leads to price spikes if the supply of transport services cannot adjust. Trade imbalances are also exacerbated by the geographical trade pattern, as only a few trade routes are being used for Malawi's cargo (figure 4.5). Certain goods

Figure 4.4 Seasonal Pattern of Exports and Imports on Key Transport Routes in Malawi, 2015

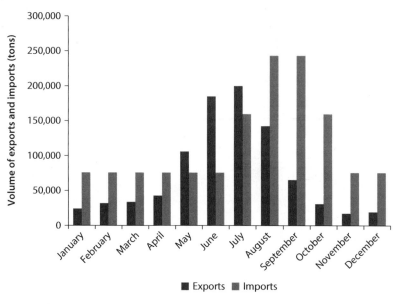

Source: Ksoll and Kunaka 2016.
Note: Covers 14 commodities.

Figure 4.5 Volume of Trade on Key Transport Routes in Malawi, 2015

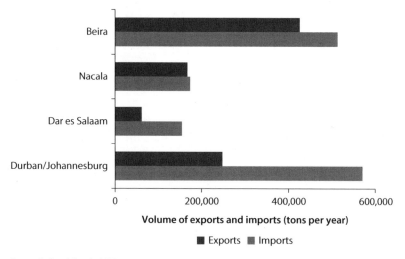

Source: Ksoll and Kunaka 2016.
Note: Covers 14 commodities.

have preferred corridors, and the segmentation of trade leads to further trade imbalances among the different corridors, especially because transport equipment is not always suitable for the return cargo (for example, fuel imports enter on tankers while agricultural exports exit in containers). Empty backhauls (as a result of imbalanced trade) are one of the key drivers of high international transport costs.

Malawian transporters face a range of difficulties in competing with foreign transporters on international corridors. For a landlocked country like Malawi, efficient transit operations and procedures are of vital importance. However, Malawi faces several domestic constraints that make it difficult to compete with transporters on international corridors, such as higher fuel prices than elsewhere in the region (except Zimbabwe), expensive spare parts and equipment (due to high import tariffs), and high costs of finance with loan rates in excess of 40 percent. Furthermore, existing supply chain structures tend to favor foreign transporters, and Malawian firms are often too small to participate in larger transport contracts. In addition, policies in Mozambique affect the smooth flow of goods between Mozambican ports and Malawi.

The Nacala railway corridor could be a potential game changer in connecting Malawi to a deep-sea port, but more needs to be done to unlock this potential. The recent improvement in rail infrastructure and systems along the Nacala corridor has addressed the single biggest binding constraint to increased use of the Nacala corridor for Malawi's trade. To promote higher volumes and greater shipping liner connectivity of the port, cargo consolidation facilities in Blantyre and Lilongwe need to be developed, coordination between the railway and port operations enhanced, and a simpler transit regime put in place.

Rural transport costs in Malawi are even higher than international costs. Domestic transport costs are much higher in Malawi than on international routes due partly to thin and seasonal fluctuations in demand, the availability of transport services, and the condition of rural roads. However, reducing rural transport prices requires more than just addressing the state of infrastructure; it requires appropriate logistics solutions, which are currently lacking.

Firms do not identify labor-related constraints such as education of workers or labor costs as a major concern. Only 11.9 percent of firms in Malawi identify education of the workforce as a major constraint, compared with 40.8 percent in Tanzania. Similarly, labor regulations concern only 4.6 percent of firms in Malawi versus 31.7 percent in Tanzania. These numbers reflect the relatively high capital intensity of Malawian firms, as few are engaged in labor-intensive sectors. However, the finding that labor is not a binding constraint does not mean that employment and education policies are of lesser importance. To the contrary, a major concern is whether Malawi's economy will be able to provide employment to the growing population with the current sectoral orientation, which also reflects low standards of education.

Limited Employment Creation

With regard to the evolution of the labor market, Malawi's demographic transition is happening at a sluggish pace. Malawi is one of the continent's most densely populated countries, characterized by high fertility rates and rapid population growth (von Carnap 2016). Malawi's population grew from 9.8 million in 1995 to 18.6 million in 2016. At current rates, the population is set to double every 23 years, and environmental and land pressures mean that such population growth cannot be absorbed in the agriculture sector. Thus, the availability of jobs at this stage of development is all the more crucial for accommodating the burgeoning working-age population.

Agriculture continues to employ the vast majority of workers, and formal employment is uncommon. Formal employment comprises only 11 percent of total employment, with a large share of own-account workers (54 percent), mostly in the agriculture sector. Around 84 percent of men and 94 percent of women hold jobs without social protection or employment benefits, which includes own-account workers as well as a large share of paid employees. According to survey data, about one in six people has a secondary job (NSO 2014). The unemployment rate has been estimated at 20 percent nationally, although this number is difficult to interpret in the context of most households being engaged in agriculture (von Carnap 2016).

Analysis of recent household surveys shows a gradual shift away from agriculture and toward employment in the services sector, although the productivity of those new jobs remains low. Recent economic growth in Malawi has had only limited effects on job creation, as it has been centered on capital-intensive industries such as mining and finance. Instead, the main driver of increased services employment has been the wholesale and retail trade sector, in which relative productivity has been declining.

Much of the employment taken up in the services sector seems to reflect coping strategies in the face of increased population pressure on agricultural land and lack of income from farming rather than the creation of new jobs with high productivity. For example, common household income-generating activities include street trading, craft services, and the sale and processing of agricultural produce. These enterprises are common among urban households (37 percent) but also prevalent in rural areas (17 percent). Their owners are significantly more likely to report an income sufficient to build savings, although the value added from such enterprises is still very low (figures 4.6 and 4.7).

With regard to labor supply, one reason for the small share of formal wage employment lies in the low levels of education. Almost two-thirds of the labor force have not completed primary education, and another 25 percent have not progressed past primary school. This is ultimately reflected in the low labor intensity of the more productive sectors, where successful companies are usually those requiring little manpower for their production or services.

At the same time, the returns to higher degrees are substantial. The returns to more education are significant even at the primary and secondary levels,

Figure 4.6 Small Household Enterprises in the Nonagriculture Sector in Malawi, by Type of Business, Fiscal Year 2010–11

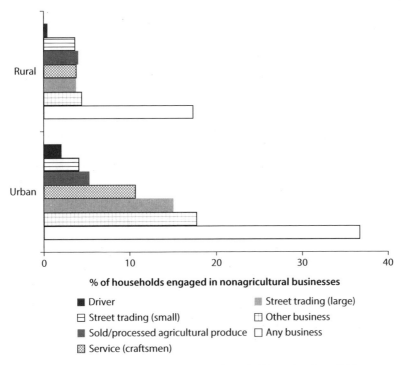

Source: Calculations based on data from the third Integrated Household Survey (von Carnap 2016).

Figure 4.7 Household Enterprises and the Ability to Increase Income and Savings, by Rural–Urban Location in Malawi, Fiscal Year 2010–11

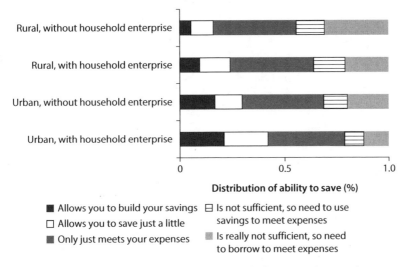

Source: Calculations based on data from the third Integrated Household Survey (von Carnap 2016).

with estimates for the latter ranging between 15 and 22 percent. This fact indicates both demand from employers and improved income opportunities for workers with even a basic level of education.

Lack of training and job-matching mechanisms make the transition from school into the workplace difficult. While firms do not view the availability and cost of adequately trained workers as major constraints, employers still complain about the unpreparedness of graduates once they enter working life. Only a few graduates benefit from established training programs, making the transition from education institutions to the workplace difficult. This difficulty is compounded by the absence of formal matching mechanisms in the labor market—a large share of companies do not use formal search mechanisms such as advertisement and public employment services, so most jobs outside of the civil service are found through personal connections.

While human capital formation remains a central policy issue, it appears that employment generation is currently held back more by demand-side constraints. After a strong period of hiring in the early 2000s, employment growth slowed to 3.2 percent a year and fell behind regional trends during 2011–13 (von Carnap 2016). Employment is mostly created in younger firms, yet companies often face difficulties in growing to scale. The demand for workers with postsecondary education is low, reflecting the scarcity of high-value jobs.

References

Ayyagari, M., M. Demirgüç-Kunt, and V. Maksimovic. 2008. "How Important Are Financing Constraints? The Role of Finance in the Business Environment." *World Bank Economic Review* 2 (3): 483–516.

Hoppe, M., and R. Newfarmer. 2014. "Using Trade to Raise Incomes for the Next Generation." Malawi Policy Note, Macroeconomics and Fiscal Management Global Practice, World Bank, Lilongwe.

Kibuuka, K., and C. Vicente. 2016. "Why Are Interest Rates So High in Malawi?" Malawi Country Economic Memorandum background paper, World Bank, Washington, DC.

Ksoll, C., and C. Kunaka. 2016. "Malawi's New Connectivity: Paving the Way for Seamless Corridors." Malawi Country Economic Memorandum background paper, World Bank, Washington, DC.

NSO (National Statistical Office). 2014. *Malawi Labor Force Survey 2013*. Zomba: Government of Malawi.

Record, R., C. Hemphill, and E. Chilima. 2016. "Malawi's Undersized Private Sector: What Are the Constraints to Higher Productivity and Increased Competitiveness?" Malawi Country Economic Memorandum background paper, World Bank, Washington, DC.

Von Carnap, T. 2016. "Creating Jobs in Malawi: Constraints to and Opportunities for an Employment Transformation." Malawi Country Economic Memorandum background paper, World Bank, Washington, DC.

World Bank. 2010. *Enterprise Surveys: Malawi Country Profile 2009*. Washington, DC: World Bank.

———. 2014. *Enterprise Surveys: Malawi Country Profile 2014*. Washington, DC: World Bank.

———. 2015. *Doing Business 2016: Measuring Regulatory Quality and Efficiency*. Washington, DC: World Bank.

CHAPTER 5

Policy and Institutional Actions for Moving Beyond "Business as Usual" to Achieve Stable and Sustained Growth and Poverty Reduction

Malawi will have to move beyond "business as usual" in order to address the challenges and constraints described in this book and to achieve stable and sustained economic growth and poverty reduction. Generally speaking, progress is needed in two respects:

- Better fiscal management overall
- Better allocation of fiscal resources to focus on areas that have the most impact on growth and poverty reduction.

Malawi needs to pursue reforms that will help to ensure macroeconomic stability, foster transformation of the agriculture sector, and encourage private sector development that provides productive income-generating opportunities for Malawi's growing population. Based on the analysis in previous chapters, this chapter lays out recommended directions for policy in four interrelated areas: macroeconomic stability, agricultural transformation, private sector development, and institutional reform. Clearly, the four proposed areas of focus are closely intertwined, and progress in one area has positive spillover effects in the others. For example, reducing deficits and volatility can help to boost private sector confidence and lower interest rates, encouraging more private sector investment, which can lead to job creation. Thus, many of the potential policies conducive to job creation fall under the wider context of macroeconomic stabilization and economic diversification. Progress in one area also depends on progress in others: without reducing macroeconomic instability, it is difficult to see how the private sector's willingness to invest will improve.

Entrenching Macroeconomic Stability

The immediate goal of the government should be to restore and entrench macroeconomic stability—a prerequisite for fostering private investment in the economy—and over the medium term to develop a track record in sound economic management. Once macroeconomic stability is entrenched, the government can give more attention to policies fostering private sector growth, which often is ignored in the midst of firefighting. Experience all over the world shows that countries need to stay the course on policy reform for years, perhaps decades, before sustainably good outcomes emerge. What matters for growth is that the private sector perceives that macroeconomic policies aim to achieve stability at all times, not just occasionally.

The government faces two interrelated challenges in the near term: (a) how to reduce fiscal deficits and (b) how to bring inflation back to single digits. To keep debt on a sustainable path, improved fiscal efforts are needed to raise primary surpluses, maintain high growth, and keep the real exchange rate flat. Large domestic debt threatens macroeconomic stability since most of it is concentrated in short-term instruments. Interest on short-term instruments changes in response to monetary policy, economic conditions outside the country, and other factors, and this uncertainty increases the vulnerability of public finances.

Strengthening fiscal management, in the areas of both budget planning and execution, is a key step to achieving stability. Malawi has sufficiently well-designed institutions for budget planning and execution. Yet all instances of economic crisis in the past have been occasions for revisiting budgetary and financial management institutions and have received strong support from Malawi's donors. Nonetheless, despite almost two decades of institutional reform, it is hard to argue, for example, that expenditure slippages will not happen again or that institutions will prevent the government from overrunning the budget or getting the Reserve Bank of Malawi to finance the deficit. Unless there is a strong political commitment to setting a realistic budget and staying within it, reforms in technical design will only be "feel-good" solutions without any real impact.

Careful prioritization of expenditures is needed to create fiscal space that would allow the government to respond to shocks without endangering macroeconomic stability. While Malawi has large financing needs across a range of sectors, it must operate within a limited resource envelope, with regard to both domestic and foreign or development finances. Resources should therefore be invested in areas where they can achieve the greatest impact. Expenditures need to be prioritized carefully, particularly if the government is to live within its means and to avoid excessive recourse to domestic borrowing. This will require difficult policy discussions around expenditure priorities, but it is the only way to move toward an economy in which inflation and interest rates can return to single digits, which is the most effective way to improve access to finance. Having more flexibility in the expenditure structure would also help to create more fiscal space as well as more space for the private sector to grow.

Ultimately, Malawi may need to reduce expenditure on a more permanent basis. Steady-state expenditure needs to be firmly linked to domestic resources rather than to the size of aid.

Increased use of fiscal and borrowing rules, if developed and owned locally, could help to establish norms regarding prudent limits on public expenditure. The adoption of a set of fiscal rules could help to establish a domestic consensus around an appropriate and more shock-resistant fiscal framework. Such fiscal rules might include, for example, a cap on recurrent expenditure linked to the amount of domestically generated resources, minimum contingency allowances in the annual budget, deficit targets over the economic cycle, and so on. However, to have an impact, such fiscal rules need to have broad ownership across government and political parties, based on a common understanding of the costs of fiscal indiscipline to Malawi's development. Similarly, a set of borrowing rules or a debt anchor could help to establish norms, perhaps by limiting domestic borrowing to short-term consumption smoothing only.

In addition, assuring central bank independence could improve the credibility of fiscal policy. Currently, the Reserve Bank of Malawi has no option but to accommodate pressures from fiscal authorities for monetizing fiscal deficits. If it has its own inflation target and is provided the institutional independence to pursue it, the Reserve Bank of Malawi may be better able to resist such pressures.

An important point is that an undiversified economic structure may be exogenous in the short run but is endogenous to governance, institutions, and policies over the long run. With weak institutions and limited policy buffers, the adverse consequences of negative shocks tend to cumulate, so low growth becomes entrenched. In addition, in such circumstances, corruption shocks like "cashgate" further reinforce the low-level equilibrium. Malawi cannot afford to mismanage domestic sources of volatility (that is, sources of volatility other than weather or changes in terms of trade). For diversification to be achieved, the country needs good infrastructure and, once again, good governance and institutions, including property and creditor rights and sustainable public finances so the private sector can take a long horizon for investing in manufacturing and services other than agriculture and tobacco.

Focusing Resources to Support Agriculture Sector Transformation More Effectively

The development vision for the agriculture sector should be one in which, working within a significantly more diversified agriculture sector overall, specialized, high-productivity farmers supply markets with the food and other agricultural products that Malawi needs. Under this vision, farmers would focus on the production of commodities for which they are best endowed and situated to produce productively and profitably, rather than producing most of the full range of agricultural commodities consumed by their household (Benson and Edelman 2016). The food security of Malawian households will therefore be increasingly assured through the marketplace rather than through own production of food. To facilitate this transformation, resources should be channeled toward interventions that foster greater diversification and commercialization of the agriculture sector, boost agricultural productivity and value addition, and strengthen agricultural markets.

To support agricultural transformation and effectively build resilience in the sector, correctly targeting public resources is as important as the size of the expenditure. Addressing many of the issues discussed earlier, such as the limited impact of the Farm Input Subsidy Program (FISP) and other agricultural support or the volatilities in the sector, requires stronger policy design and impact evaluation rather than more resources. Strengthening agricultural information systems to monitor and evaluate the implementation of policies is needed to determine whether they have the potential for scaling up or not. Building capacity for such evaluations within the ministry responsible for agriculture is also needed.

Looking at Malawi's government spending in the agriculture sector through the lens of a risk management framework, it becomes evident that a greater focus is needed on mitigating—rather than simply coping with—risks. Risk management strategies can be classified as risk mitigation, risk transfer, and risk coping mechanisms.[1] Malawi is spending heavily on coping strategies such as food aid and emergency cash transfers, while investing relatively little in mitigation strategies such as irrigation and extension services. The share of FISP in the agricultural budget rose from 47 percent in fiscal year 2006/07 to 75 percent in fiscal year 2014/15 (although this fell to less than 20 percent in 2016/17 due to restructuring of the program). A more forward-looking approach would be to invest more in building the broader resilience of the agriculture sector, thus minimizing necessary expenses in times of crises (Giertz and others 2015). Given the various challenges and risks faced by the sector, it seems important to allocate more funds for investment purposes, such as market information systems, communication and transport infrastructure, and agricultural research. Such public investments are instrumental to advancing the process of agricultural transformation.

While irrigation has been a stated key priority of the government for a long time, expenditures should be prioritized carefully. Improved water management is key to mitigating the impact of droughts and preventing destruction through floods as well as to increasing productivity. However, production of irrigated maize would only be financially viable in poor rainfall seasons or when grown in the dry season following a poor rain-fed season. More likely, having smallholders growing irrigated crops for sale in (better-functioning) markets, which would improve their financial ability to buy staples, could help to improve food security. Either way, sizable investments in irrigation require prudent management of water and soil resources (Benson and Edelman 2016). Water harvesting and improvement of on-farm practices, potentially supplemented by small-scale irrigation structures, would go a long way toward mitigating the impacts of droughts and floods and increasing productivity (Giertz and others 2015).

Although FISP has played a part in raising food production, its efficiency could be improved by better targeting more productive farmers. Scarce government resources could be used more efficiently to support the stated goal of increased maize production. The amount of fertilizer currently supplied indiscriminately to all farmers is not enough even to maintain the already low levels of soil fertility (Benson and Edelman 2016). One way to achieve better targeting would be to have farmers contribute more toward the market price—reforms in fiscal year 2015/16 raised this contribution to around 30 percent, up from the prevailing 3 percent—as this share would lead to more self-selection of those farmers who can actually profit from the inputs. Similarly, impact could also be improved by targeting farmers who have the land and labor endowments but who cannot afford fertilizer on market terms and by supporting the same beneficiaries over multiple cropping seasons.

Some reforms could help FISP to fulfill its functions in a more efficient way. Delays in the application of FISP-subsidized fertilizer due to late delivery of the input to farmers is one of the most significant inefficiencies in implementation of the program, sharply reducing its impact. Timely procurement and distribution of inputs are needed—that is, before the planting season starts—and could be accomplished by engaging private suppliers with strictly set delivery targets. In fiscal year 2016/17, private sector participation was allowed for the first time in the program's history, which improved operational efficiency, although delays were still experienced in the selection of beneficiaries and the delivery of coupons (World Bank 2017). The government should release funds for FISP before the start of the fiscal year in July to enable timely procurement and distribution of inputs well before the rains start at the end of the year. Furthermore, intercropping, crop rotation, and incorporation of organic fertilizers could complement the application of chemical fertilizer and help to restore soil fertility. The provision of incentives to farmers to combine both kinds of fertilizer and actively manage the soil could also improve overall program performance. Such incentives could include a limited duration of program participation in which farmers could use the increased yield from FISP fertilizer to invest in their farms, before graduating from the program after a certain number of years.

More transparent market behavior by the Agricultural Development and Marketing Corporation (ADMARC) would go a long way toward deepening agricultural markets and ensuring food security. ADMARC's nationwide network and transportation infrastructure continue to have an important role to play in food security and timely provision, as private markets remain underdeveloped in certain parts of the country. However, market interventions have been a source of price volatility for maize in Malawi, so it is important for any interventions to be rules-based and transparent so that information is provided on a symmetrical basis for all actors operating in the maize market. Policy makers should be cautious in allowing ADMARC to venture into other business activities and refrain from using it for political purposes. A clear set of observed rules and the adoption of set price intervention bands would encourage the participation of other private traders in the market, thus strengthening the market position of Malawian farmers and enabling them to choose from more sources of demand.

Removing export restrictions is key to encouraging investments in the maize sector. The price volatilities that Malawi experiences are a result of a closed market. Without export bans and cumbersome licensing restrictions, interventions and shocks in the maize market would have less impact on prices as the markets would adjust. Similarly, FISP or other policies would have a lesser impact on producer prices. A more stable market with higher returns would encourage much-needed investment in maize production and incentivize more commercially oriented producers.

Beyond maize, further diversification of the agriculture sector—requiring more neutral policies and support to the sector—is important for transformation and resilience. As discussed earlier, concentrating on a few crops for own production and sale makes farmers vulnerable to external shocks and affects agricultural markets across the country. Many higher-value crops are also more labor-intensive and thus more job-creating as well as income-generating. However, if FISP and other public support remains biased toward maize production in an open market, the amount of land under maize production may increase instead. It therefore is important to create a level playing field so that farmers can adapt their production to where they see the best returns for their inputs and investment.

Facilitating value addition to agricultural products would help to open up other sources of income for Malawi's predominantly rural population. The majority of agricultural produce leaves both the farm and the country unprocessed, thus generating little value and employment within the country. Increased value creation would provide additional sources of income and employment for the rural population. While rural households are commonly engaged in family-based enterprises doing small-scale processing and sale of agricultural commodities, their profitability could be enhanced by having easier access to finance and infrastructure and better linkages to potential buyers, be they final consumers, traders and exporters, or processors. Engagement of commercial operators in such processing should also be encouraged through a more conducive business environment in order to develop more integrated rural value chains.

In the absence of a sizable and dynamic domestic market, greater participation of small-scale farmers in export markets would also help to increase and diversify their incomes. With limited structural transformation away from agriculture, slow urbanization, and generally low levels of disposable income, domestic markets are unlikely to be the source of dynamic growth in demand in the near future. Economic development in the region as well as demand for niche products could present an opportunity for both the country and individual farmers to profit from international demand. However, given the high transport costs to both local and regional markets, farming strategies should focus on products with a high price-to-weight ratio to make trading and exporting economical (Ksoll and Kunaka 2016). Furthermore, sustaining a flexible but relatively stable exchange rate through lower domestic inflation would help to make Malawian exports more competitive. Oilseeds have been identified as one of the product groups potentially suitable for export-oriented production, which would mitigate some of the risks associated with Malawi's dependence on tobacco for foreign exchange earnings (Battaile 2016).

At the same time, social safety nets need to be expanded to protect better the assets of the extreme poor. Encouraging transformation of the agriculture sector means separating agricultural policy from social policy and gearing public support to the sector toward profitable, job-generating activities. An expansion of social safety nets is therefore needed to cover those parts of the agricultural population who are not able to farm maize or other commodities profitably in the current environment and who rely regularly on humanitarian aid. Providing cash rather than food aid lessens market distortions and can in fact generate demand for food and other commodities. The evidence increasingly shows that targeting cash transfers directly at the extreme poor—in particular, households who are labor- or land-constrained or both—is the most effective and cost-efficient means of protecting the poorest (Dabalen and others 2017).

While bringing down interest rates remains the key policy priority to ensure broader access to finance, expanding financial inclusion also plays an important role, particularly for rural households. Broader financial inclusion would enable consumption smoothing and facilitate self-employment in nonagricultural activities (Kibuuka and Vicente 2016). The recent initiative introducing national identification numbers is an important development that could be accompanied by an expansion in mobile banking as well as increased access to formal banking services. Improved financial literacy and financial products tailored to the needs of small businesses are also important in this respect.

Undertaking Reforms to Foster Private Sector Development and Generate Employment

Structural transformation of Malawi's economy requires not only a more efficient agriculture sector but also faster development of the nonfarm economic sector. This necessitates both removing policy barriers to private investment and job creation as well as targeting investment to alleviate key infrastructure constraints (Enache, Ghani, and O'Connell 2016).

Continuing to take a "business as usual" approach to private sector development in Malawi would leave the country stuck in a low-level equilibrium. Business as usual would mean continuing the current low-level equilibrium of private sector activity, with limited new (quality) private sector investment, low capacity utilization of existing investments, and very limited job growth (figure 5.1). It would also mean continuing to have a missing middle, with few small firms able to grow and challenge the established players. The investment climate would continue to be characterized by the outward signs of a modern legal framework but would in practice continue to wrestle with a lack of transparency and considerable uncertainty. As a result, investment would tend to be

Figure 5.1 Two Possible Scenarios for Malawi's Future Investment Climate

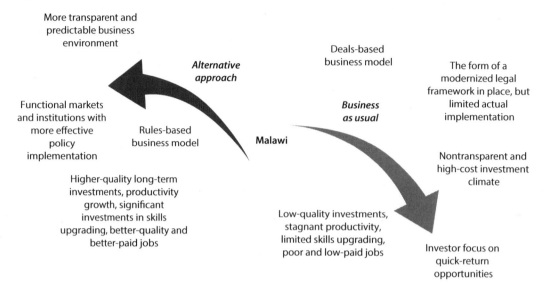

driven by a "deals-based" business model, benefiting insiders at the expense of outside competition, with investors focusing only on short-term, quick-return activities (Hoppe and Newfarmer 2014).

A better approach would be to reform radically the business enabling environment, improving transparency and predictability. The objective would be to develop an investment climate that can attract higher-quality investors and investments and facilitate the creation of more and better-quality jobs in diversified sectors. This approach would focus much less on putting in place the "form" of modernized institutions for private sector development and much more on the actual "substance" of service delivery. This may mean less use of first-best institutional solutions and more context-specific approaches that result in changes to the investment climate that can be observed at the enterprise level (Record, Hemphill, and Chilima 2016).

This new approach would require policy actions with greater emphasis on full implementation of a more limited set of reforms, rather than partial implementation in many areas. In addition to restoring macroeconomic stability and improving access to finance, the following priority steps are recommended:

- *Remove barriers to entry.* Lack of predictability and transparency in the investment climate, together with a high-cost environment and tight access to finance, make it more difficult for outsiders or new investors to enter existing markets. Lack of clarity is also a major driver of corruption and demand for gifts of informal payments by government officials (Hoppe and Newfarmer 2014). Much greater efforts are needed to make existing regulations—including tax and licensing requirements—simpler, more accessible, and easier to implement.

- *Address deficits in utility supply by facilitating private investment.* As discussed earlier, enterprises in Malawi have identified poor utility supply (electricity, in particular, but also water) as being a major binding constraint, with insufficient supply and outages raising costs and undermining productivity. Addressing this deficit should be a high priority for government policy and investment efforts. However, doing so would require deeper efforts to improve the governance of utility suppliers as well as to encourage private investment to boost installed capacity, given that the costs of filling Malawi's power and water infrastructure gaps are well beyond the available public sector resources.

- *Improve the road transport system to lower the costs of domestic and international trade.* Malawi's landlocked status and distance from markets add to the cost of trade, but domestic transport costs are also among the highest in the world. On the domestic front, a network of carefully planned rural logistics platforms should be developed around which the distribution and marketing of agricultural inputs and outputs can be organized. There is also a need to provide logistics rather than purely transport solutions to the shipment requirements of the agriculture sector. Such solutions would combine storage, road, and transport services in an optimized and comprehensive manner. On the international front, the countries of Southern Africa need to develop an integrated regional transit system. A regional approach offers many advantages over bilateral solutions but may take longer.

- *Develop infrastructure and systems to exploit the opportunity of the modernized Nacala railway corridor.* The new Nacala rail corridor offers an opportunity for Malawi to disrupt the current transport equilibrium, but complementary investments and policy reforms are needed if the country is to realize the full benefits that the corridor could provide (Ksoll and Kunaka 2016). Priority should be given to a simplified transit procedure for railways as well as investments for cargo-handling facilities in strategic locations. In addition, railway and port operations need to be better synchronized. The railway could also provide additional transport capacity to alleviate pressure on high transport prices during the harvest season for major agricultural commodities.

More generally, reducing policy uncertainty is important for fostering longer-term investments. A key barrier to investment is the uncertainty that current legislation will be changed or that barriers will be imposed in the future. Faced with policy uncertainty, investors avoid the types of long-term projects that might support higher rates of growth, job creation, and income-generating activities, for example, due to the fear that bans will be imposed on the export of certain agricultural products or that land acquisition might not be possible. Greater efforts are needed to ensure adequate consultation on policy changes, build in mechanisms that prevent ad hoc policy shifts, and address inconsistencies between the practices of different regulatory bodies.

From Falling Behind to Catching Up • http://dx.doi.org/10.1596/978-1-4648-1194-4

With regard to job creation, while policies must acknowledge the importance of the agriculture sector in poverty alleviation and food security, efforts should also be made to foster a structural transformation toward more productive parts of the economy and allow for increased urbanization. Recent research shows that urbanization can accelerate economic growth and structural change in Malawi, although increased investment in urban areas financed by own resources would need to be ensured to avoid congestion effects and the diversion of public finances from rural areas (World Bank 2016). In addition, given the widespread prevalence of secondary jobs and supplemental income sources, there may be scope for the development of rural small-scale industries and for professionalization of secondary activities to create a more diversified rural economy. Policies should focus on creating an environment in which innovative rural dwellers can access means of financing, savings, and insurance, while the infrastructure used by the rural economy is continuously improved.

Sustained investments in human capital development (that is, education and health) are of crucial importance for any such transformation to be realized. Malawi still compares poorly on educational attainment, which holds back not only the employment opportunities in existing firms but also the creation of new ones. Equitable accessibility of the education system remains crucial, and rural–urban inequality could be addressed by providing students across the geographic and social spectrum with relevant skills sought by the labor market. Providing business and entrepreneurial skills at all levels of education, from primary to university levels, would go a long way toward improving the productivity of household-based enterprises and fostering business creation by boosting the employability of university graduates. Finally, opportunities to improve matching of graduates with formal employers as well as matching of lower-skilled labor with informal or short-term opportunities should be explored to reduce periods of transition and unemployment.

Executing Reforms and Restoring the Effectiveness of Malawi's Institutions

As part of moving away from business as usual, Malawi should learn from failed reforms of the past when developing new legal and institutional reforms. A common refrain has been "lack of implementation," referring essentially to the large gap between the de jure legal and institutional framework and the de facto situation in practice. Thus, the intended results from reforms are often not achieved. An analysis of legal and institutional reforms embodied in donor projects carried out over the past 20 years in Malawi found that there is little to show for results. Numerous projects supported by development partners generated a large amount of laws, regulations, structures, and systems, yet few had a demonstrable impact on desired outcomes (Bridges 2016). Most project indicators emphasized change in how organizations *look* rather than in how they *function*.

Reforms related to economic governance are a salient example of reforms that have not worked. Malawi has a track record of adopting laws and institutional reforms that create the outward semblance of a modernized system of economic governance but do not address the underlying issues. This "partial reform syndrome" manifests in repeated crises, followed by newer reforms that again fail to address the underlying problem. Indeed, the 2013 "cashgate" crisis threw into stark relief the fundamental and deep-rooted problems in economic governance in the Malawi government that have remained largely impervious to public financial management reforms for two decades.

An important reason for the failure of reforms could have been inappropriate technical design. It is possible that the technical design of many of these institutional reforms was not adapted to the Malawian situation. Reformers could have failed to construct and deconstruct the initial problem adequately or to explore it in its full complexity and then applied best practices with little regard for preexisting institutions and rules. Researchers have identified several reasons for taking a solution-driven, best-practice approach rather than a problem-solving approach. These include a culture of preprogramming ("locked in" solutions), professional pressure and government demand for "best-practice" reforms, and a skill set among donor staff that is more suited to providing solutions than to analyzing problems. The best-practice approach also confers local and global legitimacy on both those who advocate and those who adopt it.

For complex challenges with many unknowns, the government could consider problem-driven, adaptive, or agile approaches to reforms. These approaches emphasize focusing on specific *problems* prioritized by local actors; fostering active, ongoing *experimental iterations*; establishing an "authorizing environment" for decision making that encourages experimentation; and engaging a *broad set of agents* to ensure that reforms are politically supportable and practically implementable (figure 5.2).

Political incentives behind economic policy and management (commonly referred to as *political economy*) are an even more important reason for the failure of reforms. Political scientists have argued that Malawi's policy arena is characterized by both the legacies of past political and economic strategies that bet on a limited set of private sector partners to deliver growth and rents as well as the current electoral dynamics that favor short-term clientelist strategies over long-term investment in public goods. Historically, policies favoring agricultural estates delivered growth and rents that underpinned the elite bargain but failed to deliver broad-based dividends, leaving the majority of the population in vulnerable subsistence farming. As external conditions, compounded by internal policies, undercut growth, short-term rents dried up, weakening the patronage system and leading to political competition. In turn, politicians have been incentivized to focus on shoring up support through clientelist strategies that deliver select private goods at the expense of longer-term development policies (Said and Singini 2014).

Figure 5.2 Solution-Driven Approach

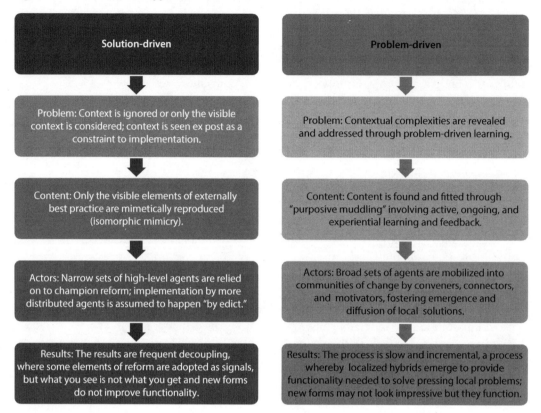

Source: Bridges and Woolcock 2016.

These cycles have created a persistent low-level equilibrium that constrains the state's ability to commit to stable macroeconomic fiscal policies, to invest in a meritocratic and capable bureaucracy, and to coordinate public and private actors to implement systematic measures to prevent (rather than react to) food insecurity. Instead, they have perpetuated a political logic in which corruption is tolerated as a means of rewarding loyalists, and rents are captured to promote political aims rather than to reinvest in poverty reduction and inclusive growth (Cammack, Kelsall, and Booth 2010).

Heavy aid dependence also distorts political incentives for reforms. A considerable literature argues that heavy dependence on aid distorts political incentives in low- and middle-income countries. Arguably, donor policies contribute to the persistence of failed reforms by conditioning aid on superficial reforms rather than on reforms that functionally enhance state commitment and collective action capacity.

Ultimately, serious progress on the four areas of focus identified in this book— macroeconomic stability, agricultural transformation, private sector development, and institutional reform—requires overcoming Malawi's deep political economy trap. Politicians need to break from past and current patterns of patronage politics and seek to establish a more inclusive political settlement that aligns elite incentives with developmental ends. This is a real challenge in the regionally fragmented political environment in which many elites strongly benefit from the status quo. Citizens can accelerate this path to the extent that they can organize collective action that holds politicians accountable for implementing good policies. This too is difficult given the low levels of education and pervasive poverty that make the promise of short-term benefits appealing. Development partners have a role to play as well in targeting aid in ways that enhance commitment, strengthen contestability through increased transparency and accountability, and incentivize outcomes and not just laws and forms. Box 5.1 depicts a schematic of an approach to policy making that takes into account the interests of all those affected by policy changes.

Box 5.1 Lessons for Malawi from the *World Development Report 2017*

The *World Development Report 2017: Governance and the Law* (*WDR*) addresses the question of why, despite knowing what policies are technically required, governments may fail to adopt or implement them and why first–best policies may fail to achieve their intended goals (World Bank 2017). The WDR argues that policy effectiveness is a function of governance—that is, the process by which actors with different relative power and incentives bargain over the ways in which resources, responsibilities, and rights are distributed in what it calls "the policy arena." Who has a seat at the table and what their incentives are is determined by both de jure rules as well as de facto, informal norms shaped by the interaction between socioeconomic conditions and the evolution of political institutions. To the extent that the policy arena is characterized by the exclusion of key groups, by the dominance of certain elites who capture policies to promote their narrow interests, or by clientelist strategies whereby elites "buy" their hold on power, it will be difficult to deliver on policies in the general public good. Specifically, short-term interests of maintaining power and stability may limit the ability of governments to commit credibly to longer-term policies and to induce coordination and cooperation among those policies needed to implement change.

The WDR presents a framework for looking at how power asymmetries affect the policy-making process. As the framework diagram in figure B5.1.1 shows, the relationship between outcomes, which shape power, and the production of policies is both closely linked and persistent (right side of the diagram). However, it is not static. History is full of instances in which societies have improved rules, institutions, and processes that have helped them to move closer to reaching their development goals (left side of the diagram).

The WDR argues that change happens by shifting the incentives of those with power, reshaping their preferences and beliefs in favor of positive outcomes, and taking into account

box continues next page

Box 5.1 Lessons for Malawi from the *World Development Report 2017* (continued)

Figure B5.1.1 Framework for Looking at How Power Asymmetries Affect Policy Making

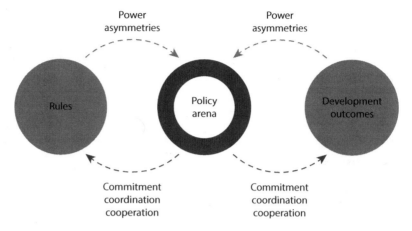

the interests of previously excluded participants, thereby increasing contestability. These changes can be brought about as a result of shocks or through gradual structural changes that reshape power relations and the incentives of the elites who strike power bargains, through greater citizen engagement, as well as through international actors whose efforts can influence the relative ability of domestic coalitions to push for reforms.

Note

1. Risk mitigation refers to actions taken to eliminate or reduce the probability of events or to reduce the severity of losses (for example, water-draining infrastructure, diversification). They can be seen as investments with inherent returns that are potentially even higher during crises, when measured as averted losses. Risk transfer places potential risk on a willing third party at a cost (for example, insurance, financial hedging). Risk coping refers to actions that help to cope with the losses caused by a risk event (for example, government assistance to farmers).

References

Battaile, W. 2016. "Diversifying Malawi's Exports: A Product Space Brief." Malawi Country Economic Memorandum background paper, World Bank, Washington, DC.

Benson, T., and B. Edelman. 2016. "Policies for Accelerating Growth in Agriculture and Agribusiness in Malawi." Malawi Country Economic Memorandum background paper, World Bank, Washington, DC.

Bridges, K. 2016. "Why the Iceberg Sinks—A Critical Look at Malawi's History of Institutional Reform." Malawi Country Economic Memorandum background paper, World Bank, Washington, DC.

Bridges, K., and M. Woolcock. 2016. "How (Not) to Fix Problems That Matter: Assessing and Responding to Malawi's History of Institutional Reform." Policy Research Working Paper, World Bank, Washington, DC.

Cammack, D., T. Kelsall, and D. Booth. 2010. "Developmental Patrimonialism: The Case of Malawi." APPP Working Paper 12, African Power and Politics Programme, Overseas Development Institute, London.

Dabalen, A., A. de la Fuente, A. Goyal, W. Karamba, N. Viet Nguyen, and T. Tanaka. 2017. *Pathways to Prosperity in Rural Malawi*. Directions in Development. Washington, DC: World Bank.

Enache, M., E. Ghani, and S. O'Connell. 2016. "Structural Transformation in Africa and Malawi: A Historical View." Malawi Country Economic Memorandum background paper, World Bank, Washington, DC.

Giertz, Å., J. Caballero, M. Dileva, D. Galperin, and T. Johnson. 2015. "Managing Agricultural Risk for Growth and Food Security in Malawi." Agricultural Global Practice Note 15, World Bank, Washington, DC.

Hoppe, M., and R. Newfarmer. 2014. "Using Trade to Raise Incomes for the Next Generation." Malawi Policy Notes, Macroeconomics and Fiscal Management Global Practice, World Bank, Lilongwe.

Kibuuka, K., and C. Vicente. 2016. "Why Are Interest Rates So High in Malawi?" Malawi Country Economic Memorandum background paper, World Bank, Washington, DC.

Ksoll, C., and C. Kunaka. 2016. "Malawi's New Connectivity: Paving the Way for Seamless Corridors." Malawi Country Economic Memorandum background paper, World Bank, Washington, DC.

Record, R., C. Hemphill, and E. Chilima. 2016. "Malawi's Undersized Private Sector: What Are the Constraints to Higher Productivity and Increased Competitiveness?" Malawi Country Economic Memorandum background paper, World Bank, Washington, DC.

Said, J., and K. Singini. 2014. "The Political Economy Determinants of Economic Growth in Malawi." ESID Working Paper 40, Effective States and Inclusive Development Research Centre, University of Manchester, Manchester.

World Bank. 2016. *Malawi Urbanization Review: Leveraging Urbanization for National Growth and Development*. Urban, Rural, and Disaster Risk Management Global Practice. Washington, DC: World Bank.

———. 2017. *World Development Report 2017: Governance and the Law*. World Bank Group Flagship Report. Washington, DC: World Bank.

List of Background Papers

Preparation of the Country Economic Memorandum was informed by a large amount of background research, with detailed findings from this work included in a series of background papers.

Policies for Accelerating Growth in Agriculture and Agribusiness in Malawi
Todd Benson and Brent Edelman

Malawi's Undersized Private Sector: What Are the Constraints to Higher Productivity and Increased Competitiveness?
Richard Record, Carter Hemphill, George Clarke, and Efrem Chilima

Malawi's Growth Performance in a Historical Perspective: Implications for Future Growth Strategy
Priscilla Kandoole, Eleni Stylianou, and Tillmann von Carnap

Growth Policies for Malawi, Rwanda, and Uganda
Shahid Yusuf and Praveen Kumar

Why the Iceberg Sinks: A Critical Look at Malawi's History of Institutional Reform
Kate Bridges

Why Are Interest Rates So High in Malawi?
Katie Kibuuka and Carlos Vicente

Creating Jobs in Malawi: Constraints to and Opportunities for an Employment Transformation
Tillmann von Carnap

Diversifying Malawi's Exports: A Product Space Brief
Bill Battaile

Structural Transformation in Africa and Malawi: A Historical View
Maria Enache, Ejaz Ghani, and Stephen O'Connell

Malawi's Tax System: Issues and the Way Ahead
Tuan Minh Le and Priscilla Kandoole

Malawi's New Connectivity: Paving the Way for Seamless Corridors
Christian Ksoll and Charles Kunaka